The big book *of* brain-storming games

Quick, Effective Activities That Encourage Out-of-the-Box Thinking, Improve Collaboration, and Spark Great Ideas!

Mary Scannell & Mike Mulvihill

RECEIVED
MAY 17 2012
OCEAN COUNTY COLLEGE LIBRARY

McGraw Hill

New York Chicago San Francisco Lisbon London Madrid Mexico City Milan New Delhi San Juan Seoul Singapore Sydney Toronto

The McGraw·Hill Companies

Copyright © 2012 by Mary Scannell and Mike Mulvihill. All rights reserved. Printed in the United States of America. Except as permitted under the United States Copyright Act of 1976, no part of this publication may be reproduced or distributed in any form or by any means, or stored in a database or retrieval system, without the prior written permission of the publisher.

1   2   3   4   5   6   7   8   9   10   QFR/QFR   1   9   8   7   6   5   4   3   2

ISBN 978-0-07-179316-2
MHID   0-07-179316-X

e-ISBN 978-0-07-179317-9
e-MHID   0-07-179317-8

Trademarks: McGraw-Hill, the McGraw-Hill Publishing logo, The Big Book of, and related trade dress are trademarks or registered trademarks of The McGraw-Hill Companies and/or its affiliates in the United States and other countries and may not be used without written permission. All other trademarks are the property of their respective owners. The McGraw-Hill Companies is not associated with any product or vendor mentioned in this book.

McGraw-Hill books are available at special quantity discounts to use as premiums and sales promotions or for use in corporate training programs. To contact a representative, please e-mail us at bulksales@mcgraw-hill.com.

Illustrations by Drake Carr.

This book is printed on acid-free paper.

MAY 1 7 2012

OCEAN COUNTY COLLEGE LIBRARY

Contents

5 Active Paradigm Shifts   69

6 It's a Storm, Not a Drizzle   83

Acknowledgments

Thank you to the groups who have allowed us into your brainstorming sessions to observe your processes, your challenges, and your brilliance!

Thank you to our team at McGraw-Hill, which includes one of the best editors around, Donya Dickerson. Your expertise and support throughout this process was invaluable. Thank you to Julia Baxter and Sara Hendricksen for promoting our Big Books in a Big Way! We would also like to express our sincere appreciation to Rena Copperman and her team, who help make the production process flow smoothly every time. To Carolyn Wendt, our eagle-eye copyeditor, thanks for all the great "catches."

A special thank you to our exceptional illustrator, Drake Carr, who adds vitality to our games with his creative drawings. We are lucky to have found someone who can really make the pen dance with his artistic talents.

On a personal note:

I am extremely grateful to my family and friends for their encouragement and enthusiasm during this process and throughout my life. To my mom, Alice, a one-woman brainstorming whirlwind! You inspire me every day. To my dad, Ed, for challenging me with countless brainteasers over the years and especially for your "yes, and" approach to life. To Karen, Mike, and Cathie, for your insight and guidance. To the "festing" crew, for your love, laughter, and support. And to Kerry, my own personal Renaissance man, thank you for challenging me to consider the other perspective and to think differently.

Mary Scannell

I've been fortunate throughout the years to be surrounded by an incredibly creative bunch of friends and colleagues, all of whom have encouraged and inspired me along the way. My love and gratitude go out to all of you. I would like to thank the many teams I've had the pleasure of working with, and the facilitators I've learned from and been inspired by throughout my career. A special thanks to my coauthor, Mary Scannell, for all the hard work, laughter, and creativity that went into the making of this book.

I would also like to thank my family for their encouragement during the writing of this book. What a great cheering section you have been! And how lucky I am to have all of you in my life!

Finally, I would like to thank my wife Chrissy for her love, friendship, and support. You mean the world to me.

Mike Mulvihill

1

The Weather Forecast Calls for Brainstorming

Brainstorming has probably been around as long as people have had problems and the ability to communicate. Although we don't have specific data to back this up, fire came about as a result of brainstorming. How could it not? When you have a clearly articulated problem, "We're cold," or "We need to cook our wildebeest," and a group of creative individuals ("We can do this; after all, we came up with the wheel"), who understand and follow the principle of "Ug Ug (Yes! and . . .)," brainstorming is the perfect technique.

Brainstorming in its truest sense is intended to be a practical approach to problem solving.

While the technique has been used for a long time, the term *brainstorming* is relatively new. Flash forward to 1953. Advertising executive Alex Osborn, in his book *Applied Imagination*, first expressed to the masses how a well-run group of people could generate more ideas than the same number of individuals thinking on their own. The word *brainstorm* was coined in 1939 by a team led by Osborn. According to Osborn, "Brainstorm means using the brain to storm a creative problem and to do so in commando fashion, each 'stormer' audaciously attacking the same objective." This quote sums up Osborn's perspective on creative thinking, "It is easier to tone down a wild idea than to think up a new one."

The brainstorming principles Osborn suggested are simple:

- Focus on quantity instead of quality.
- Allow no criticism.
- Welcome far-fetched ideas.
- Build upon each other's ideas.

Though there is some uncertainty that brainstorming works for every team in every situation, there is no denying that collaboration yields greater results than individual thinking. Brainstorming is a way a team can come together and generate ideas. There are additional techniques, but we recommend using the original four principles no matter what technique you choose.

Let's consider the four principles—focus on quantity, allow no criticism, welcome far-fetched ideas, build on each other's ideas—and how they not only generate ideas in a brainstorming session, but also can help build an amazing team. A team who understands the rules, grasps the reasons for the rules, and is committed to following the rules becomes a high-functioning team, whether they are in a brainstorming session or just carrying out tasks and interacting on a normal workday.

The four principles or rules become the way in which the team members relate to each other.

- A focus on quantity gives your team an "abundance" mentality. Why should we withhold information and compete? There is plenty for everyone. Changes coming our way? We can handle it; we have an abundance of skills and knowledge to transform, bend, or switch direction if necessary.
- Allow no criticism. What kind of environment would you create if team members were not criticized for their ideas? A team who lives this rule is a team who looks for the good in others or the upside in a situation. If our natural, or learned, tendency is to support, we will engage in dialogue to understand, instead of debating to win. We will provide feedback in a way that is respectful and helpful. Because we look for the good in the other people on our team, we have no need to backstab or become passive-aggressive. Rather than become resentful, we are happy for others' accomplishments.
- Welcoming far-fetched ideas promotes creativity and diversity on your team. We associate ourselves with our ideas, so if we welcome far-fetched ideas, we welcome differences. Your team members are supportive, encouraging, and respectful of one another.
- When we live the rule, "Build on each other's ideas," we become better listeners. And we listen *for* rather than *against* the other person on our team. We bring a "Yes! and . . ." approach to whatever we do. We become more aware of team members and how we can bring out the best in each other. We build a team with a high level of trust.

The games and activities in this book will help you run more effective brainstorming sessions. The games and activities in this book will also help you build a better team.

Brainstorming

Today, brainstorming seems to be a catchall word for a group of people coming together and throwing out ideas until the boss chooses the best one. Somehow along the way, we have lost the essence of brainstorming, and as a result, we are losing out on some brilliant ideas because of it.

How do we get the essence of true brainstorming back? A good place to start is with an understanding of why it works, how it works, and a belief that it will work for your group.

Why Brainstorming Works

When you combine a clear problem-statement with the unique interpretation, understanding, perspective, background, knowledge, and experience of each individual participant, you leverage a collective set of opinions, thoughts, ideas, and potential solutions. Whew!

Brainstorming works because we each have different perspectives through which we examine problems. These different viewpoints can provide an infinite number of ideas. It provides an environment to encourage the ideas and ultimately inspire more ideas.

Brainstorming allows a team to achieve the best possible results by combining all available resources. It can fast-track the gathering of information and ideas because every person in the session adds value to the outcome. Many significant contributions come about when all input is welcome and no idea is discarded.

How Brainstorming Works

First, start with a clear problem-statement or goal to provide direction. The more concise the statement, the easier it is for the group to understand the issue and come up with ideas. Sometimes articulating exactly what the issue is can be a challenge. Like all the other techniques in this book, you can get better at it with practice.

Most of us are not very comfortable with unstructured, anything-goes, free-form idea-generating sessions. To get the most of brainstorming sessions, provide a structure to allow for creativity. The structure, used consistently, will help participants become comfortable with the process, to understand what is expected, and to understand their specific responsibilities. Just because you are looking for wild and crazy ideas does not mean your session has to be a free-for-all.

An effective way to provide some structure is to use a technique such as the SCAMPER method, developed by Bob Eberle. SCAMPER is an acronym for seven thinking strategies that help groups generate more ideas:

Substitute—components, materials, people.

Combine—join two or more elements.

Adapt—change some part of the problem so it works where it didn't before; change the function.

Modify—make it bigger or smaller; change the shape, color, or other attributes.

Purpose—modify the purpose; put to another use. Think about what it's supposed to do or what it's typically used for and challenge any assumptions.

Eliminate—simplify, remove any or all elements; reduce to core functionality.

Reverse—make it go upside down, inside out, or in reverse. Make it go in the opposite direction from the one originally intended.

At any point in a creative-thinking situation, present the SCAMPER strategies to force the group to think in a different way (this technique works with individuals, too). You can use any or all of the approaches suggested by the technique. When using the SCAMPER method, keep the principle of "force fitting" in mind. If the team can't think of anything right away when presented with the particular prompt you've chosen, force a response—any response—no matter how illogical the idea is. It's easier to tone down a ridiculous idea than to bolster a lackluster idea.

How to Make Brainstorming Work for Your Team

Make sure all participants have an understanding of what brainstorming is and isn't. Make sure they comprehend the basic principles and are willing to be held accountable for following the basic principles or any additional brainstorming norms the team has developed (the game Storm Norms, page 25, will help you with this). Make sure they warm up their brains before getting into the real brainstorming. Finally, make sure they have time to think individually before the session by providing them with the brainstorming topic ahead of time.

Have a facilitator run the brainstorming session. Many group members are hesitant to throw out bold, unusual, or unconventional ideas in front of their direct superior. Choose a neutral facilitator to encourage the participants and to enforce the rules.

Leaders can lay the groundwork for a high-performance brainstorming team by creating an atmosphere of trust and modeling a sense of fun and discovery. Leaders should remind team members that mistakes are a natural part of the process. They should also stress that the ideas are more important than the individuals.

Chapter 2 goes into more detail, but here are some fundamentals that work for all teams:

1. Begin with warm-up exercises to get everyone's minds moving in the right direction, similar to the idea of warming up before participating in a sporting activity.
2. Give a clear statement of the problem.
3. Make sure everyone understands the problem.
4. Make sure the problem is not too complex (if it is, break it down).
5. Make sure you have the right number of people. Alex Osborn suggested a group size of between five and ten people. That gives you enough raw material to generate lots of ideas and ensures you don't have too many people so that you lose out on some ideas.
6. Have rules.
7. Make the rules fun.
8. Post the rules.
9. Make sure everyone follows the rules.
10. Have fun!

With some planning, and a team that understands the principles, brainstorming can take you places you never thought possible.

2

How to Run Your Brainstorming Session

A great brainstorming session doesn't happen by accident. It takes plenty of preparation to create an experience that is fun, focused, and results-oriented. As the person running your session, take time to learn about what it takes to make your session a success.

Before the Start of Your Session

Define your brainstorming topic. This will bring focus to the process. It's important for every member of the group to know exactly what they will be brainstorming about. Make sure it's something specific: a single idea that can be simply stated. Here are some examples:

- Develop three new features for our product.
- Speed up the time it takes to ship orders.
- Find ways to save costs without cutting staff.
- Attract customers to our grand opening.

A clearly defined topic is like a good road map, showing group members where they need to go. Without it, your group may flounder or feel as if they're talking in circles without getting anywhere. Having a clear picture of where to go will help keep the conversation on track and ensure that everyone's energy is going in the same direction.

Pick your brainstorming team. A diverse cross section of people is best. Don't pick a bunch of people who think the same, or you'll end up with a bunch of ideas that seem the same. You can brainstorm with any number of people, but we recommend five to ten people for optimal results. A group that's too small will not bring enough breadth of perspectives and won't provide enough opportunities to feed off each other's ideas. A group that's too large will be hard to manage, and ensuring that everyone is heard from will be too time consuming. As a result, people may check out from the process, get bored, or feel left out.

Decide who will facilitate the session. People may hold back crazy or bold ideas in front of their boss. Bosses, don't lead the session! An outsider, such as someone from a different department, may be best. An outsider can be more neutral than a team member or boss. Sometimes it pays to bring in a professional facilitator.

Give group members a premeeting assignment. A 2010 study by researchers at the Wharton School at the University of Pennsylvania found that brainstorming teams who first give members time to come up with ideas on their own, followed by working together as a group, will generate more and better ideas, and be able to evaluate their ideas better. ("Idea Generation and the Quality of the Best Idea," Girotra, Terwiesch, & Ulrich, *Management Science 56*:591–605.)

Call or email everyone to let them know the topic of your brainstorming session. Encourage them to brainstorm by themselves first, without discussing the topic with anyone else. Do this the day before the meeting, giving them time to think about their topic and allowing their ideas to incubate. Tell them to jot down at least three ideas and bring their list to the meeting. At the start of the meeting, group members can present their list of ideas themselves, or everyone's ideas can be submitted anonymously and posted or read aloud by the facilitator.

Brainstorming Preparation List

To boost your group's ability to generate great ideas, create an atmosphere that will stimulate people's minds and engage their senses. Prior to your brainstorming session, stock your meeting room with items that will get people thinking creatively. You'll also want to have on hand all the things you'll need to record those good ideas.

The items in this list are geared to help make your brainstorming session fun and creative. Remember that by making your session fun, group members will think more creatively, participate more fully, and generate more ideas than they would in a standard, boring meeting.

- **Colorful sticky notes.** An ample supply of colored sticky notes of assorted sizes is an essential part of the brainstorming toolbox. A good practice is to have group members jot down one thought or idea per sticky note. Small notes work best for written words, while medium-size notes are great for doodles or sketched ideas. After your group has brainstormed about their topic, have them post their sticky notes on a wall or whiteboard for everyone to see.

Encourage the group to play with and explore their ideas by moving and rearranging their sticky notes. For example, notes can be grouped into clusters of similar ideas, arranged to create a linear time line, or moved to different parts of the wall or whiteboard based on various themes ("customer-focused ideas," "time-saving ideas," etc.). The ability to move and rearrange notes can reveal underlying patterns and increase the possibility of more insights or a better understanding of your topic.

- **Pens, colored markers, crayons.** Give your group lots of ways to record their ideas. Assign different colors for different brainstorming topics or themes. Use jumbo markers for big important ideas or to emphasize solidity or permanence. Use thin, fine-point pens to record more detail-oriented ideas.

- **Notepads.** Use letter- or legal-size notepads to record individual group members' ideas.

- **A dry-erase whiteboard, flip chart, and/or easel pads**. These large-size meeting essentials are ideal for recording and displaying your group's ideas.

- **Butcher paper.** A table covered with butcher paper is an inviting canvas for your team's ideas. Less formal and more inviting than a whiteboard or easel pad, a big sheet of butcher paper lets people write their ideas in large, exaggerated script, sketch or doodle their creative thoughts, or build on someone else's ideas in a fun free-form way. Lots of people can gather around at the same time. Encourage group members to jot their ideas as they are happening, even if they aren't fully formed yet. Don't let them wait until their idea is fully baked to jot it down! The flow that comes from in-the-moment writing and doodling can be just the thing that spurs new ideas.

- **Magazines, coffee-table books, mail-order catalogs, or other photo or graphic-rich publications.** These types of publications can be a rich source of inspiration during your brainstorming session. Try to link the words or images to your topic in unexpected ways, or use them to spark new ideas. For example, a nature magazine photo of an elephant may bring to mind the notion of strength or power. In what ways can the subject of your brainstorming be strengthened or made more powerful? It's said that an elephant never forgets. In what ways can you make the subject of your brainstorming session unforgettable? Symbolized by an elephant, the Hindu god Ganesha is known as the remover of obstacles. What obstacles or unnecessary features can be eliminated or removed from your brainstorming subject? Try adapting the style of a magazine ad to your topic. What do the words and pictures convey?

Style? Luxury? Economy? Adventure? Comfort? Safety? Does the ad take a minimalist approach, using few words and just one or two well-chosen images to capture an idea or convey a feeling? In what ways can your brainstorming subject be boiled down to its bare essentials? Does the ad or photo contain lots of detailed information about its topic, explaining or showing readers everything they need to know about the product or service? Have you thought through all the details and many facets of your brainstorming subject? Are there aspects of your subject that still need to be explored?

- **Play-Doh, Tinkertoys, Legos, or other building toys.** Colorful, tactile building toys like Play-Doh, Legos, and Tinkertoys invite group members to adopt a playful mindset of creativity and discovery. Sculpting and building toys like these allow for a hands-on exploration of the group's brainstorming topic and can help group members find new ways to define their challenge or clarify what's most important about their product, service, or process. For example, a group concerned with creating a better TV remote control can create a mock Play-Doh version of it, using different colors or super-sizing parts of the remote control to emphasize its most important features. For a fun brainstorming activity that features Play-Doh, see Playable Clayables on page 191.

- **Digital camera.** Helpful for capturing a whiteboard covered with sticky notes, pages from a flip chart, or a sprawling idea-covered piece of butcher paper, digital photos can be shared easily with group members via e-mail, team message board, or company intranet. Digital photos are a great way for participants to recall and build on the highlights of the brainstorming session. They can also be useful in bringing group members who could not attend the brainstorming session up to speed.

- **Stopwatch or timer.** Use a countdown timer for short, intense bursts of rapid-fire brainstorming. Challenge your group to generate 15 ideas (or whatever goal you choose) in three minutes. See how the pressure of a time deadline can push your group to generate even more ideas. You'll find a huge number of stopwatch and timer apps that can be installed on your iPhone, Android, BlackBerry, or other mobile device. A good old-fashioned kitchen timer or stopwatch will also do the trick.

- **Music player.** Create a vibe that's conducive to brainstorming by including music in your next session. Pick music that's high energy and motivating, or music that's calming and meditative. See where different types of music lead your group creatively. Try including some world music to broaden your perspective and take your ideas in new and exciting directions. How about classical music? Listen as J. S. Bach creates and explores endless variations of a musical theme, then let his music inspire you to create and explore variations on your brainstorming theme. Check out Music to Soothe the Savage Team on page 21, Garage Band on page 119, and Doodle Round, Doodle Sound on page 123 for creative ways to include music in your brainstorming session.

- **Computer, Laptop, iPad, or other web-connected device.** Jump-start your own creative process by viewing an inspiring talk from an innovation leader on TED.com. Watch a few funny TV commercials on YouTube. Or take advantage of the many free creative-thinking or mind-mapping websites like bubbl.us or mind42.com to help you collaborate and generate ideas more effectively.
- **Beverages and snacks.** Ideas flow best when minds and bodies are nourished. In addition to decreasing one's energy level, being hungry can be a distraction. Hungry group members may end up focusing on watching the clock, counting down the minutes until break time. Provide a variety of sweet and healthy snacks and a selection of beverages. Some people swear by caffeine as a brain booster and must have their coffee or soda, while others prefer other options like bottled water, iced tea, or fruit juices.
- **Comfortable seating.** Arrange seats and tables in a circle or horseshoe shape to create an informal atmosphere where full participation is encouraged.

During Your Brainstorming Session

Start with an Icebreaker

Start your brainstorming session on a positive note by including a brief icebreaker activity. Establish a lighthearted tone. Put people at ease with a get-to-know-you activity. Build trust. Set a climate of fun and engagement. See Chapter 3, "Climate-Setting Activities," for some fun icebreakers.

Establish Ground Rules

Take some time establishing guidelines that group members will follow during the session. It will be important for the success of your session to choose ground rules everyone agrees upon. Put them in your own words if you wish (see Storm Norms on page 25). Make them fun, use playful termi-nology, and post them in creative fonts.

A good starting point is Alex Osborn's four original principles of brainstorming:

1. **Quantity instead of quality.** The goal is lots of ideas. Don't evaluate or screen out any ideas. That will happen in a later phase, but not now. This is the time to be idea-generating superheroes! Your group's ideas may come in waves, with lulls in between. Don't stop when the first lull happens—keep going! More ideas will come.
2. **No criticism allowed.** People will shut down and clam up if their ideas are shot down.
3. **Encourage wild and exaggerated ideas.** Ideas that may seem crazy can often trigger a whole new volley of ideas from the rest of the team and may lead to your best solution ever.
4. **Build on each other's ideas.** Now's the time for everyone to check their egos at the door and give up some control.

Assign a Team Scribe

Assign someone from the group to be your Team Scribe. This person's role is to record everyone's ideas, making sure to note them as accurately as possible. It is important that your Team Scribe remains neutral during the brainstorming process. He or she should refrain from offering opinions, filtering anyone's ideas, or changing the original intent of the contributor.

Prime the Pump

Before you begin brainstorming about your actual topic, prime everyone's creative pumps. Make it fun. Brainstorm about something unrelated to your topic, just to get in the flow of generating lots of ideas. Use an activity from Chapter 4, "Priming the Pump," to get started.

Put Ideas First

In a good brainstorming session, ideas *always* come first. Not egos. Not one's position in the organizational chart. Not office politics. Ideas.

Good ideas can come from anyone, not just the boss or the usual "creative thinkers" of the group. Remind group members not to cling to ownership of their ideas. Once an idea is spoken, it belongs to the group. If you contribute an idea, do your best to answer your teammates' questions or clarify your vision for the rest of the team. Once you have done this, let the idea go.

The Facilitator's Role

As facilitator, you play a key role in the success of your brainstorming session. Your job is to keep the ideas flowing, to encourage the participants, to validate the process, to track the ideas so the brainstormers don't get distracted by writing, to enforce the rules, and to keep track of the time.

A good facilitator is like a symphony conductor. A conductor listens to all the sounds of the orchestra to make sure all the musicians play in harmony. The conductor pays attention to the tempo, keeping time, and making sure to maintain the pacing, not letting things slow down, or speed up too fast. A good conductor notices if the brass section is playing too loudly and signals the players to quiet them down. If the string section is playing too softly, the conductor will signal them to play louder.

During your session, try to imagine yourself as a conductor. You will need to maintain the pacing of the meeting, encourage quiet participants to speak up more, and signal loud or dominant group members to tone it down so that everyone can contribute.

Qualities of a Good Facilitator

- Unbiased
- Supportive
- Encouraging
- High energy
- Willing to keep the focus on the goal or problem
- Able to hold the team accountable for following the rules
- Great listener

3

Climate-Setting Activities

The creation of a thousand forests is in one acorn.

—Ralph Waldo Emerson

Music to Soothe the Savage Team

OBJECTIVES
- To generate different ideas
- To increase creative thinking

Group Size

Individual or groups of up to 20 people

Materials

Laptop, PC, iPod, CD player or other media player with external speakers

Time

20 to 30 minutes

Procedure

Music can be a powerful tool for brainstorming. It has the power to inspire us, change our mood, pump us up or calm us down, or even challenge our way of thinking. Whether brainstorming by yourself or with a group, knowing what music works best to stir your creative process and provide inspiration can prove valuable.

Select the music and create your playlist prior to the start of your meeting. Skipping between selections too rapidly will distract group members, so be sure to let each musical selection play for at least five minutes.

Pay attention to what happens within your group as you move from one musical style to another. Watch for the way each selection affects the group's creative output, the number of ideas generated, the group's energy level, and so on. You may discover that certain types of music work better for your group than others. If a certain style or piece of music seems to work for your team, that's great!

Don't stop there. Experiment with all sorts of different music during your meetings. Avoid playing only music that the group likes. It may be helpful to let everyone know that the purpose of this exercise is to give them an opportunity to step outside their normal way of seeing things (or in this case, hearing things) and be open to new ideas. Like many of the other exercises in this book, creative ideas often happen when people step outside their comfort zones.

Tips

For each meeting, assign a different person to be their music "explorer." Request that they find new and different music that will be a surprise for everyone.

I'm an Acronym

OBJECTIVES

- To jump-start the creative process
- To form a deeper connection with the team

Group Size

Up to 15

Materials

None

Time

10 minutes

Procedure

Tell the participants you are going to have everyone do some quick introductions. Everyone is going to treat his or her first name as if it is an acronym. Give them three to five minutes to decide what they will assign for each letter of their name. For example: MIKE could be Mighty, Interested, Kind, Encouraging.

Variations

Have team members introduce each other using this method. Participants are usually complimentary in this version, so it ends up being a way to recognize another member of the team and deepen the connections.

Tips

As the facilitator, be prepared to start the process with your acronym.

Storm Norms

OBJECTIVES

- To create norms and expectations for the team's current and future brainstorming sessions
- To get buy-in of brainstorming guidelines from all participants

Group Size

3 to 20

Materials

Alex Osborn's rules of brainstorming (provided), flip chart, paper, pens

Time

20 to 30 minutes

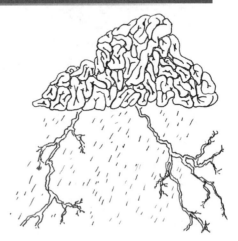

Procedure

The most productive brainstorming takes place when everyone understands the process involved. Research shows that the people who understand the process of brainstorming yield better results than those groups who don't understand the rules. To get the most from your sessions, it's good for your team to understand what brainstorming is and is not. At the very least, it's essential for the person conducting the brainstorming to have a solid understanding of what brainstorming should be. This exercise is designed to help every team member become familiar with the basics of brainstorming. The activity is based on the rules of brainstorming described by Alex Osborn. It allows the team to establish their own way of interpreting Osborn's rules and to adapt them in a way that is mutually agreed upon by the team.

To start the process, write out Alex Osborn's original rules of brainstorming and post them in a prominent place:

- Generate lots of ideas.
- Allow no criticism.
- Welcome wild and crazy ideas.
- Build on each other's ideas.

Tell the group that they will be creating "Storm Norms." Storm Norms are guidelines and rules created by the team that specify how they conduct their brainstorming sessions. To create their Storm Norms, they will use Osborn's original rules as a starting point, adding new rules and adapting the original rules in a way that will make the most sense for their team. Have the group discuss each of Osborn's rules one at a time, asking the following questions:

- Why was this included as a rule?
- Why is this rule important?
- What is the benefit?
- What does that look like for us?
- How can we hold ourselves and our team accountable for following this rule?
- How can we state this rule using our own words?

Here is a sample script:

"Let's put the rules into our own words. If there are some of our own ideas to add, let's do that too. What ideas do we need to highlight based on how we work together? If it seems that any of these rules are especially relevant to our group, let's highlight those ideas so that we can all see the importance of the rules. If our group has a tendency to shoot down ideas, it may be a good idea to emphasize the rule 'no criticism allowed.' What rules stay? How should they be adapted? What rules need to be added?"

In essence, you are asking the team to brainstorm about brainstorming. Here are some examples of what you may hear from the team during this activity:

- Generate lots of ideas: *Why*? Lots of ideas give more to choose from. Why shouldn't the group stop when you hear a good idea? Good ideas can lead to great ideas!
- Allow no criticism: *If an idea is clearly bad, why do we need to hold our tongues?* A bad idea can lead to a good idea. It can trigger thoughts in another team member that may lead to a good idea. A "bad" idea can also help a group get out of a rut, putting it on a different line of thinking that may be fruitful. On an interpersonal level, we squash a person's input when we shoot down his or her ideas. An individual whose ideas have been shot down will be more likely to clam up and less likely to contribute to the group.
- Welcome wild and crazy ideas: *Wild ideas will never work here! Why are crazy ideas good? Why throw out a crazy idea, when you know it will never be used? What are the risks of throwing out a crazy idea? What can a team do to ensure that crazy ideas are welcome? What's the value of a crazy idea?* All good questions to consider. It's easier to tone down a wild idea than build up a mediocre idea.
- Build on each other's ideas: *Hey, but I want all the credit!* If some feel that their ideas are perfect, how willing are they to allow the team to build on them? How does trust play to this? What are some ways to build on ideas? When do we stop?

Variations
If your group is ten or fewer, have everyone work on this together. For larger groups, split them in half; have each team work on its norms, then come together to look for commonalities and agree on the guidelines.

Tips
Create a list of the team's newly created Storm Norms and exhibit the list in all future brainstorming sessions.

The Big Cheese

OBJECTIVE
- To generate energy and excitement

Group Size

At least 15 people, working in teams of 3

Materials

None

Time

10 to 15 minutes

Procedure

Invite each team to assign each of their team members one of three leadership roles:

- The Big Cheese
- The Head Honcho
- The Top Dog

Tell the team that this game is played in three two-minute rounds, and that each person will play the role of leader during one of the rounds. When in the role of leader, they will have the chance to assign tasks to the other two people to be carried out immediately. Take a look at the Sample Tasks that follow for some ideas. The commands should be fun and easily and quickly carried out. Once the two team members have completed the task, they come back to the leader for a new job. The game is intended to be played fast and furious.

The positive energy and excitement that each team generates during this quick activity will linger long after and help the group feel more comfortable and more creative while building connections they can tap into throughout the brainstorming session.

Sample Tasks

- Tell everyone with brown hair that their hair is looking especially lovely or handsome that day.
- Compliment anyone who is taller than you about their shoes.
- Find the youngest person in the room, then describe the ways he or she reminds you of Albert Einstein.
- Sincerely thank every brown-eyed person in the room for being here today.
- Give a wink to anyone who brought his or her laptop.

Variations

Have the teams come up with their own creative names for the three different leaders.

Discussion Questions

1. How can we maintain a high level of energy during brainstorming sessions?

2. What can you do differently to increase your energy level?

3. What can you do to increase the energy level of other team members?

I'm Impressed!

OBJECTIVES
- To practice creativity
- To lighten the mood and have some fun

Group Size

Up to 12 people

Materials

Paper and pens

Time

10 to 20 minutes

Procedure

Tell the team that they will be introducing the person on their right to the rest of the group. The idea is to come up with the most outlandish and exaggerated introduction they can come up with. The only thing that needs to be factual is the person's name. For example, "To my right is Bob Smith. You may know Bob as the person who invented the Internet in 1985. Bob is an avid rodeo bull rider who also maintains the world's largest collection of Beanie Babies. Bob takes pride in the large tattoo of the nation of New Zealand that covers his back. Bob has an IQ of 160, which is rare for a supermodel."

Provide paper and pens and allow a few minutes for them to jot down some ideas. Group members will have up to one minute to present their introductions. Go around the room with the introductions, laughing and applauding their creativity.

I Doodle, Do You?

OBJECTIVES
- To improve creative skills
- To appreciate diverse perspectives

Group Size

Any, split into teams of 6 to 8

Materials

One I Doodle, Do You? handout, pens for each participant

Time

10 to 15 minutes

Procedure

Pass out one copy of the I Doodle, Do You? handout to each participant. Allow five to ten minutes for everyone to complete the doodles on the page. After everyone is finished, have them show and compare their drawings to those of the other members of their team. It's fun and interesting to see different perspectives of the same starter squiggles.

Variations

For a different version, pass out one index card to each person and ask that they draw a line, shape, or squiggle on the card. You can provide an example similar to the starters used on the handout to give them an idea of what you are looking for. Everyone passes their card to the right and completes the drawing started by the other person. Have everyone show their drawings when completed.

Discussion Questions

1. How many completed drawings did you have in common with others in the room? Why or why not?

2. How is this activity similar to the brainstorming process?

3. How can we ensure we get diverse perspectives when we brainstorm?

4. What can we do to encourage ourselves and our team to be more creative?

I Doodle, Do You?

Drawing	Your Completed Doodle
1.	
2.	
3.	
4.	
5.	

Find the Sweet Spot

OBJECTIVES

- To discover the communication styles of your brainstorming teammates
- To create a deeper level of trust within the group

Group Size

Any

Materials

Blue painter's tape or two 20-foot lengths of rope, one paper plate or similar item

Time

15 to 30 minutes

Procedure

Place a length of rope or tape on the ground and tell the group that the rope or tape represents a specific trait: how they prefer to process information (this is an example; you can choose a different trait or characteristic that may apply more specifically to your team). Say to the team:

"Everyone processes information differently. Some people are external processors to the extreme. They love to chat, talk, chew the fat, discuss, and debate with as many people as they can. At the opposite end of the spectrum, some people are internal processors. They will cogitate, meditate, reflect, ponder, and consider the problem from all angles, preferable all by themselves.

"Where do you stand? If you are an extreme internal processor, stand at that end of the rope. If you are an extreme external processor, stand on the opposite end of the rope. If you are somewhere in the middle, position yourself accordingly."

Once everyone has positioned themselves on the first rope, lay out the second rope so it crosses the first, making a "X" and creating four quadrants.

Now tell the team:

"This new rope indicates another trait: how flexible and open to new ideas you consider yourself. One end of the rope represents someone who is very flexible and open; the other end of the rope represents someone who is inflexible and maybe a little stubborn. Now we have two additional traits to consider. For example, where would someone who is very flexible and an external processor stand? Please place yourself in one of the quadrants, standing in a spot that most accurately represents where you are in relation to these two traits."

Go around the team and have everyone explain why they chose to stand where they are. Now, as a group, challenge them to identify the group's "sweet spot." This is the position on the grid that the group feels will allow

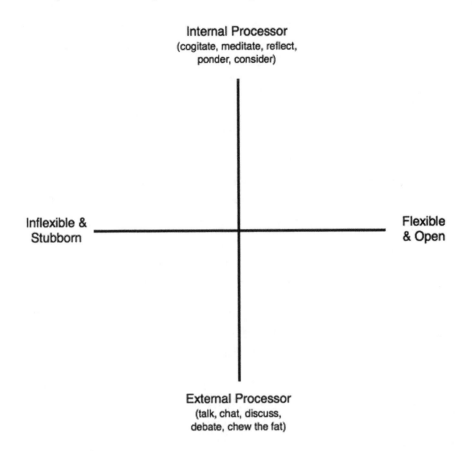

them to be most productive—their ideal spot. Have the team place a marker on that spot (use a paper plate). Then have the team talk about what it will take to get them there.

Variations

Feel free to use different continuums, which will lead to different discussions and can help a team clarify what's important to them. Here are some examples:

- Concrete vs. Abstract
- Simple vs. Complex
- One way vs. Many paths
- Fuzzy rules vs. Clear-cut rules
- Process vs. Outcome
- Intuitive vs. Analytical
- Team success vs. Individual glory

Discussion Questions

1. How well rounded is our team based upon where everyone stands?

2. What can you learn from someone who is in the opposite quadrant?

3. What are some ways we can get to our sweet spot?

4

Priming the Pump

I began by tinkering around with some old tunes I knew. Then, just to try something different, I set to putting some music to the rhythm that I used in jerking ice-cream sodas at the Poodle Dog. I fooled around with the tune more and more until at last, lo and behold, I had completed my first piece of finished music.

—Duke Ellington

Bad Ideas Welcome! Part 1

OBJECTIVES

- To overcome the fear of bad ideas
- To maximize the number of ideas generated
- To eliminate people's tendency to self-edit their ideas

Group Size

Any

Materials

An everyday item like a coffee cup, mobile device, or shoe; whiteboard or flip chart and markers

Time

10 to 15 minutes

Procedure

Group members will sometimes hold back ideas or suggestions in a brainstorming session out of fear of being singled out for a bad idea. In this exercise, team members are encouraged to contribute bad ideas with no consequence or fear of failure. This prime-the-pump activity helps set a tone where all ideas are welcome, and it gives the added benefit of sharing some laughs together with your team.

For this activity, pick any prop to brainstorm about—a cup, a book, a mobile phone, or anything nearby. Have team members call out as many "bad" ideas as possible about the item. Bad ideas can include making the item from a different material, using the item for unintended purposes, adding extra nonessential features, and so on. Give the group five to ten minutes to generate a list of 25 ideas. If the group is on a roll, let the activity go longer. Select one person to be the team scribe and write all the ideas on the whiteboard or flip chart. Every person in the group should contribute as many ideas as they can think of.

Example: Coffee Cup

- Make holes in it.
- Make it out of cement.
- Add scratch and sniff with gross smells.
- Make it out of tissue paper.
- Add a label that reads: Brewed with 100% reclaimed water.
- Paint it with lead paint.

Knowing what something *should not* be helps clarify what it *should* be.

As facilitator, try to create a lighthearted tone that encourages everyone to join in. Remind the team that in real brainstorming a bad idea spoken aloud can help trigger a great idea from another team member.

This activity will generate some funny ideas as well as some truly awful ideas. The point is that team members will want to join in the fun and contribute without holding back.

Follow-Up Activity

This activity uses a generic prop (coffee cup, etc.) to get things going. We suggest following up with the activity called Bad Ideas Welcome! Part 2, on page 85, which applies the same technique to your group's real-life situation. Again, brainstorming about what something should not be helps clarify what it should be.

Discussion Question

1. Why is it easier to generate a list of bad ideas?

10-20-30

OBJECTIVES
- To energize participants prior to their "real" brainstorming session
- To experience how a challenge can inspire the group to be more creative

Group Size

Any; split larger groups into teams of 4 to 6

Materials

Stopwatch, paper and pens

Time

12 to 15 minutes

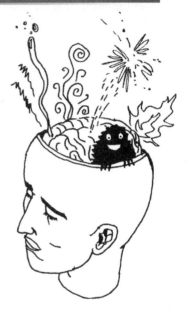

Procedure

This activity really primes the pump for teams and gets them in the mode of rapid-fire, unself-conscious idea generation. Use it as a lead-in to a real brainstorming session. The directions are easy, and the energy created will carry well into your real brainstorming session. Split large groups into brainstorming teams of four to six people. Give them the challenge—the topic and the time limit—and say "go!"

- Give the teams two minutes to brainstorm ten ideas about a fun, unusual, or "real" topic. Call time at exactly two minutes, and have teams report out on their total number of ideas.
- Then give the teams four minutes to brainstorm 20 ideas about a different topic. Call time at exactly four minutes and get their totals for this round.
- Then give the teams six minutes to brainstorm 30 ideas about a completely different topic. Call time at exactly six minutes and have teams report on their total ideas for this round.

Examples of topics include: What can you use a paper clip for? Styrofoam cup? Paper plate? Pipe cleaner? Paper grocery sack? It's fun to have these props around as well. Having the physical prop helps visualize different uses.

Tips

If you have two or three smaller teams, have team members switch up the teams for each round.

Three Random Words

OBJECTIVES
- To understand the concept of combining ideas
- To practice withholding judgment

Group Size

Any

Materials

Slips of paper—enough for at least three per person, pens, a bag

Time

10 to 20 minutes

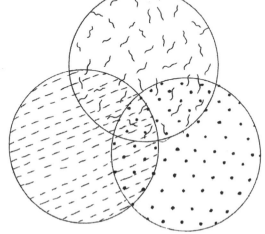

Procedure

This fun activity gives brainstorming groups a chance to develop their ability to combine concepts, which is a classic brainstorming technique. Generating and combining ideas is at the heart of brainstorming.

To start the game, give each group member three small slips of paper, and instruct them to write one word on each slip. The words should be vivid, unusual, and unrelated. For example, *kitten, bazooka, fizzy.* Remind team members to keep everything in good taste for the workplace.

After all group members have recorded their words, collect them and place them in a bag. Now comes the fun part. Pass the bag to one brave volunteer. That person reaches into the bag and selects three slips of paper without looking. He or she must come up with a sentence or mini-story that combines all three words.

For example, "My kitten always seems to get into mischief. The other day, she knocked over my soda, resulting in a fizzy mess. As a result of her bad behavior, I sent her off to military school, where she learned, among other things, how to fire a bazooka."

This is best for groups that are comfortable with each other and may not be suitable for teams that are still getting acclimated to each other and the brainstorming process.

Continue until all group members have had a chance to choose three slips of paper and tell their story.

Variations

For new groups, you can easily adapt this game using the team approach. One person selects the three words, and the whole team crafts a sentence or story together.

Discussion Questions

1. Did you notice your ideas came more freely when the spotlight was not on you but another person?
2. Have you ever experienced, the "I should have said that!" feeling after a brainstorming session? How can we make sure we get all the ideas during the discussion?
3. What would be a plan to capture ideas that team members think of "after the fact"?

Creative Combos

OBJECTIVES

- To increase creativity
- To experience combining ideas

Group Size

Up to 12

Materials

One paper grocery sack and assorted common office supplies, such as a stapler, adhesive tape, marker, paper clip, ruler, highlighter pen, sticky notes, staple remover, and paper. Have enough items so there is one for each person.

Time

10 minutes

Procedure

Combining is an effective brainstorming technique that entails taking two seemingly unrelated items and combining them in a creative way. It can be a great way to increase the number of ideas generated in your brainstorming sessions.

This game introduces the combining technique in a fun and nonthreatening way. To start, place all the items in the paper bag before everyone arrives. One at a time, pass the bag around the team and have each person put his or her hand into the bag and grab one item. Have each one pull it out and show the rest of the group. Now this person needs to explain how the item relates to him or her. Combining this person's personal characteristics with the features of the office supply he or she has chosen from the bag, ask how the item describes his or her work style. What qualities or characteristics does the individual have in common with the item?

Have each person start with the prompt: "My work style is like this _____ [stapler, marker, sticky note, etc.] because _____."

Variations

Rather than combining personal characteristics with the object from the bag, have the team focus on the team's characteristics. You can use the prompt: "Our team is like this _____ [stapler, marker, sticky note, etc.] because _____." Track the ideas and when you are done, you have a list of all the reasons your team is great!

Put It in Reverse

OBJECTIVES
- To gain a different perspective
- To prime the pump for your brainstorming session

Group Size

Any

Materials

One Put It in Reverse handout per group

Time

20 to 40 minutes

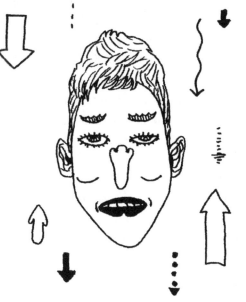

Procedure

In groups there is the always the threat of "groupthink" when the members are more interested in gaining the approval of others, rather than coming up with creative solutions. Fresh ideas are minimal when everyone thinks alike.

Reversing our viewpoint is a great way to build creativity and improve thinking. Every once in a while, it's interesting to observe the mental changes that take place when we disagree with ideas, principles, or beliefs we would normally find acceptable. When we consider an opposing viewpoint as our own, we gain perspective, and we open our minds to new and different ways of thinking.

Next time your group's creativity is lacking, use this method to challenge their creative muscle and break through the conformity barrier. Frame the technique in a lighthearted way—you can even use the words "Let's take a minute and put it in reverse to see what we come up with," to preface your disagreement. Then take one of the ideas and turn it on its head, think of it in reverse, or work it backward.

You can even apply this concept with individual brainstorming by asking a colleague or teammate to take the opposing viewpoint. When you request an opposing, viewpoint, you are usually more open to listening to understand, rather than to listen in judgment. Who knows, you may find that the opposite view makes more sense.

To practice this technique with a team, pass out one copy of the Put It in Reverse handout to each small group of four to six people. Ask them to pass the handout around the group so each person can circle one virtue they normally live by or agree with. Then allow ten minutes for groups to go through each of the circled virtues and consider the reverse viewpoint and present the opposing argument. There is an example at the top of the handout to get them started. Request they take notes throughout their discussion. When the ten minutes are up, give groups an additional five minutes to discuss three things they learned or considered differently as a result of the activity. Follow with your brainstorming session.

Variations

If you don't have anyone to disagree with you, why not try disagreeing with yourself? Doing this individually is a great way to "turn it on its head."

Put It in Reverse

Take the opposing viewpoint for these commonsense proverbs.

For example: "First things first." It's great to consider where you want to end up and work it backwards. Asking yourself "what's it going to take to get there?" helps clarify an action plan. You also can gain a sense of control over the process. Now you try it: Take one of the commonsense proverbs provided below and put it in reverse:

- Business before pleasure.
- Every cloud has a silver lining.
- Don't put all your eggs in one basket.
- Curiosity killed the cat.
- Beauty is only skin-deep.
- A bird in the hand is worth two in the bush.
- First things first.
- He who hesitates is lost.
- Early to bed and early to rise makes a man healthy, wealthy, and wise.
- If at first you don't succeed, try, try again.
- Do unto others as you would have them do unto you.
- Look before you leap.
- Experience is the mother of all wisdom.
- Fight fire with fire.
- Don't count your chickens before they are hatched.
- Patience is a virtue.
- Do as I say, and not as I do.
- Better to dine alone than in bad company.
- Diligence is the mother of good fortune.
- Better late than never.
- A chain is only as strong as its weakest link.
- Every dog has its day.
- You can't teach an old dog new tricks.

- The squeaky wheel gets the grease.
- Lightning never strikes twice in the same place.
- All work and no play makes Jack a dull boy.
- Too many cooks spoil the broth.
- Those who live in glass houses shouldn't throw stones.
- Don't cry over spilled milk.
- Make hay while the sun shines.

Wild and Crazy Animals

OBJECTIVES
- To warm up before the real brainstorming begins
- To engage in some fun, creative thinking

Group Size

Any, split into teams of 3

Materials

Slips of paper, writing paper, pens, paper bag or small box

Time

15 to 20 minutes

Procedure

To get the group accustomed to using the basic rules of brainstorming (generate lots of ideas, no criticizing allowed, build on each other's ideas), give them this mini brainstorming challenge. The first step is to have each person write the name of an animal on a slip of paper. Have them fold the paper in half. Go around the room and collect all the slips of paper and place them in a paper bag or small box.

Next, split your group into teams of three. Any additional participants can either act as observers, or you can have a couple of teams consisting of four people.

Have each team pick two slips of paper from the box. If they get a duplicate animal, have them put one back and pick a new slip with a different animal.

Tell teams they have ten minutes to brainstorm to invent a new animal based on the combination of the two animals they drew from the box.

Because brainstorming is about coming up with lots of ideas, their new animal should contain lots of details. Require each team to come up with the following:

- What is the new animal called?
- What does it look like? (illustration required)
- What are its characteristics?
- What does it eat?
- Where is its natural habitat?
- What sounds does it make? (Please demonstrate for the rest of the group.)

Remind group members of the rules of brainstorming. It's a good idea to post the rules so that everyone can refer to them throughout the process. When they are done, have each team present their animal to the rest of the group.

Discussion Questions

1. What techniques did you use while you were brainstorming?

2. How did those techniques benefit the outcome?

3. Were there any techniques you didn't use? Why?

4. Overall, what are some ways these traditional brainstorming rules help us generate creative solutions?

5. What are some ways we are willing to be held accountable to follow the rules when we brainstorm?

6. What are some respectful ways in which we can provide feedback when a team member ignores the rules? (For example, makes a comment such as, "That's impossible," or "Yes, but what we really should do is . . .")

Dubious Definitions

Objectives
- Jump-start people's creative thinking skills
- Warm up before your real brainstorming begins

Group Size

Up to 10

Materials

Dictionary, slips of paper and pens, a bag, small box or other container

Time

10 minutes

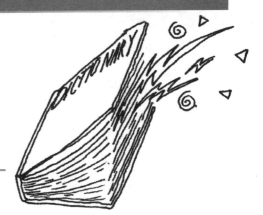

Procedure

Pass out slips of paper and pens to everyone. Take turns finding obscure words in the dictionary. Have one person find a word and then read the word, but not its definition, aloud to the rest of the group. Next, have each group member invent a convincing-sounding definition for the word and write it on a slip of paper. While the rest of the group is making up their invented definitions, the person who selected the word from the dictionary should write the true and actual definition on his or her slip of paper.

The person who selected the word from the dictionary should collect all the definitions in a small container. He or she should mix up and then read aloud to the group all the definitions, including both the made-up ones and the actual one. He or she should take care not to disclose to the group which is which.

Next, go around the table and have each group member guess the definition they think is the actual one. Group members who guess the correct definition earn one point. Any member whose made-up definition is chosen earns two points for a "bluff" well done.

Play this game for ten minutes, or longer if the group is having fun. When time is up, give the person with the highest score a big round of applause. Your group is now ready to begin the real brainstorming session.

Ultimate Nine-Dot Challenge

OBJECTIVES
- To challenge ourselves to think differently
- To consider other perspectives when brainstorming

Group Size

Any

Materials

One copy of the Ultimate Nine-Dot Challenge handout for each participant, pens

Time

10 to 15 minutes

Procedure

Pass out the Ultimate Nine-Dot Challenge handout to each group member. Give everyone a few minutes to work on the handout individually, and then allow them to work in small teams of three or four people. After five minutes, have the small teams share their solutions with the whole group. If any of the four challenges have not been solved, give everyone five additional minutes to brainstorm other solutions as one large group.

Discussion Questions

1. Were you able to change your way of thinking during the challenge?
2. What helped you change your perspective?
3. How is this beneficial during the idea-generating stage of brainstorming?
4. What are some ways we can incorporate these strategies into brainstorming sessions?

Ultimate Nine-Dot Challenge

Connect all nine dots with five straight lines without lifting pen or pencil off the paper.

Connect all nine dots with four straight lines without lifting pen or pencil off the paper.

Connect all nine dots with three straight lines without lifting pen or pencil off the paper.

Connect all nine dots with one straight line without lifting pen or pencil off the paper.

Ultimate Nine-Dot Challenge

Answers

Connect all nine dots with five straight lines without lifting pen or pencil off the paper.

Connect all nine dots with four straight lines without lifting pen or pencil off the paper.

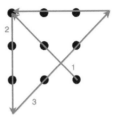

Connect all nine dots with three straight lines without lifting pen or pencil off the paper.

Connect all nine dots with one straight line without lifting pen or pencil off the paper.

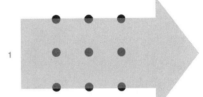

The Two Men

OBJECTIVES
- To build lateral thinking skills
- To put group members into brainstorming mode

Group Size

Any, split into teams of 5 or 6

Materials

One copy of The Two Men handout and pens for
each team

Time

10 minutes

Procedure

Lateral thinking puzzles are a way for your group
to warm up their brains to different ways of thinking. Lateral puzzles typically don't contain much
information and may have a variety of solutions,
although there is usually one solution that fits
the facts a little better than the rest. Using these types of games allows the
group to practice their brainstorming skills in a fun and challenging way.

Break your group into teams of five or six participants. Have each team
assign one of their members to act as observer during the activity. Inform
this individual that in the role of observer, he or she won't be actively participating in the activity, but must pay attention to the group dynamics that
happen while their team brainstorms to find a solution to each puzzle.

Give all the teams a copy of The Two Men handout and some pens to
help work out the solutions. Tell the teams to discuss the two scenarios on
the handout and come up with an explanation regarding each scenario.
Let them know that the scenarios are independent of one another and that
each has one unique solution that makes the most sense. Teams will have
15 minutes to discuss both scenarios and write down their answers.

Several more lateral thinking puzzles are available on the Internet. It's fun to see how the group improves their creative-thinking skills as time goes on.

Tips

Lateral thinking puzzles are easy to find on the Internet, so say to the group, "In the spirit of the game, please keep your electronic devices out of play."

Spoiler Alert! Answers follow.

Answers

The Man in the Elevator: The man is a little person. He can reach the first-floor button to get to the ground floor, but he can only reach as high as the seventh-floor button, so he must walk the extra floors to get to his apartment on the tenth floor. Variations of this puzzle include the clue that on rainy days he goes up in the elevator to the tenth floor (he uses his umbrella to punch the button for the tenth floor).

The Man in the Bar: The man had hiccups. The bartender recognized this from his speech and drew the gun in order to give him a shock. It worked and cured the hiccups—so the man no longer needed the water.

Discussion Questions

1. What are your solutions?

2. What was effective in your approach to solving the problems?

3. What could you have done differently?

4. In what ways does it benefit a team to brainstorm solutions?

5. Are you curious about the "real" answers?

The Two Men

1. The Man in the Elevator

A man lives on the tenth floor of a building. Every day he takes the elevator to go down to the ground floor to go to work or to go shopping. When he returns, he takes the elevator to the seventh floor and walks up the stairs to reach his apartment on the tenth floor. He hates walking, so why does he do it?

2. The Man in the Bar

A man walks into a bar and asks the bartender for a glass of water. The bartender pulls out a gun and points it at the man. The man says thank you and walks out.

Grab and Go Brainstorming Tips: Great Big Juicy Words

Here is a list of words to help you if you or your group is stuck in a creative rut. All of these words on this list have been handpicked for their "juiciness," that is, their ability to evoke vivid images and ideas. Pick any word from this list, either at random or just because it looks juicy to you. Then figure out how your word connects, solves, or relates to your problem.

apple suitcase socks bottle window wastebasket comb pocket bullet hook chain wheel shoelace book ketchup star smoke bed cup paper strap box tape pot printer cord frame magnet leash button slippers chair rug ladder shelf bench soap bucket shovel plant tornado cloud lion bumblebee family bicycle art flag trophy window picture bacon candy shredder track scissors journal race-car ruler foam mirror ant sun ball triangle soup ocean backpack bandana light-socket sunrise subway odor horseshoe stick case circle wrench paperclip lamp candle bear shelf beach umbrella snorkel tank tea panda water algae elephant watch ring ear eye spot minivan automobile carpool neighborhood cubicle dinosaur logo swing kettle blockbuster name tag watch slide fork snake crayon cheese steamboat football pepperoni zombie pit bull flamethrower detective racehorse palm tree polish prisoner lightning chip hole starburst raft washer waterfall oven post cocoon head spice halo pepper boat anvil shovel glue rabbit foot straw ambulance lightning television boots measles casserole medal hairpin bridge rust football tattoo armpit dress bedroom vault searchlight castle metronome seed octopus chamomile tie drain plug boat iceberg crosswalk word pin vampire piano poison bubble-bath toothbrush pumpkin pie scorpion steamroller wallet telescope straight jacket canoe mariachi crutches nursery whiskey tumbleweed masterpiece furnace camera fast-food paint spam flower flute razor-blade seashell diamond ring wound mousetrap ditch pistol feather movie star sermon yoga monkeywrench harpoon rainbow charcoal shipwreck explosion robot utensil rod goalpost easy chair hotel vacuum cash kitten pen flight attendant icicle bull's-eye school bus turntable ear blog bedtime-story mermaid building cookie-dough steam harpoon windmill mullet corral green light wrestler shack cancer cowbell waiter blanket mouthwash sandals calculator oil vitamin orchestra seat surfboard rock star chicken blood cactus cupcake taxicab tweet blindfold gearshift window electric guitar giraffe circuit wiffle ball onion keyboard note Ferrari cotton-candy lantern dishwasher lobster doggie bag championship unicycle jet pack forest gasoline grapevine garbage-can gloves costume hairbrush javelin hymnal anchor media donut urine bullhorn carcass cheese mountain tree sailboat cowboy hat gravel thumbtack bowling ball bumblebee microchip lava assassin bread tinderbox hammer skunk baseball bat shark carrot carnation corpse bandwidth mallet eagle helmet massage janitor waffle lawn-mower cigarettes whistle matchstick hunter alien jellyfish caviar reindeer cocktail merry-go-round cannon fur coat stockmarket guitar turtle 18-wheeler rump-roast monster carton projector boulder party harmonica sushi library anvil champagne coffeepot junkyard satin sheets smooth jazz trapeze table barbell wink pickle prune frosting basement ball-cap skeleton curlers binder birdcage book pinball puzzle goalpost touchdown monocle peanut wheelchair mosquito-bite Internet wi-fi mustard tortilla lasso mirror coach nap road-map daydream wart slice stop-sign dragon inchworm cruise stake marathon rock album robot tunnel altar diamond army computer bag tide bank weed cell cesspool compass circle code web dress current detour ear button face factory fairy fan farm feather fertilizer field finger engine floodlight foam weapon farm amoeba anvil bait balloon hinge horse image junk knot algebra alphabet child lamp leg liquid manual match data base menu prison monster muscle microscope rainbow rudder safe sauce saloon shadow shovel smoke skeleton room treadmill oven sphere wand square filter root temple star valley fruit library purse molecule battery armor fountain bed seed maze water air earth money spice bell rash horizon ice index key ladder landslide lever lock machine map mattress meteor mist moon music net ocean sphere pore prison pyramid record river rope rug sand saw screw shell signature nail meter missile motor organ nose onion palette pebble star vise lake lens milk mask medal lightning mountain needle vertebra violin powder

5

Active Paradigm Shifts

Genius is one percent inspiration, and ninety-nine percent perspiration.

—Thomas Edison

Warp Speed

OBJECTIVES
- To engage in creative problem solving as a group
- To involve everyone in the brainstorming process
- To experience how having a challenging goal can spur creativity

Group Size

8 to 16 people

Materials

A tossable object like a beanbag, tennis ball, or small stuffed animal

Time

15 to 20 minutes

Procedure

Starting in a circle, group members must pass a beanbag, tennis ball, small stuffed animal, or other tossable item from one person to the next. The first person selects someone in the group to toss the object to. The tosser should announce the receiver's name to alert him or her to be ready to catch the object. Using an easy-to-catch underhand throw, the passer will then toss the object to the receiver.

Upon catching the object, the receiver will select a new person to toss to, announcing that person's name prior to tossing it to him or her. The group should continue in this way until every member has had a chance to send and receive the object. Everyone should only toss and receive one time. The last person to receive the object will complete the circuit by tossing it back to the person who started it. Tell the group to remember to whom they threw and to whom they received from so they can repeat the pattern.

Have the group repeat the circuit, this time setting a speed goal they think will be challenging yet doable. They will follow the same person-to-person pattern as before. Designate one person to be the official timer.

Once they succeed in reaching their speed goal, challenge the group to cut their time in half. Give them a few minutes to brainstorm ways to go faster before they make their attempt. Let them have a few tries to reach the new goal.

Finally, challenge the group to achieve the seemingly impossible Warp Speed time of two seconds or less.

To achieve Warp Speed, the group must brainstorm creatively, building on one another's ideas. Group members may find that they must change their way of doing things to be successful.

Here are the rules:

1. The group must complete the circuit following the same person-to-person pattern as before. They can, however, rearrange where they stand. (They do not need to stay in a circle.)
2. The clock starts at Go! and ends when the object finishes back with the person who started.
3. Only one person at a time may be in contact with the object.
4. If the object touches the ground at any time, the team must start again.

Discussion Questions

1. How did having a challenging time goal affect your "creative output"?
2. Let's consider the original brainstorming principles: Generate lots of ideas, no criticizing allowed, welcome wild and crazy ideas, and build on each other's ideas. Can you think of some examples of your group using the principles during this game?
3. Based on your experience, in what ways do the original principles help produce a better brainstorming session?

Mental Handcuffs

OBJECTIVES
- To illustrate the power of a breakthrough idea
- To experience how problem definition can impact brainstorming

Group Size

Any

Materials

One 6-foot rope for each person

Time

10 minutes

Procedure

This is a tough challenge. It's not uncommon for no one to figure it out. Don't let that dissuade you from using this activity, because it has very insightful lessons that relate beautifully to creativity and "out-of-the-box" thinking.

To begin this activity, invite the members of your group to find a partner. Next, pass out one piece of rope to each person. From here on out, refer to the ropes as "handcuffs." To make the handcuffs, take the ropes (six-foot-long segments of ordinary cloth utility rope—the kind used for clotheslines), and tie a loop at each end of the rope. Make sure the loops are large enough for someone to slide their hand through.

Ask that one partner place one hand in each of the loops of his or her handcuffs. The second partner places just one hand in a loop of his or her handcuff and then passes their handcuff over the partner's handcuffs before placing his or her second hand in the remaining loop. At this point both partners will have their hands in their own handcuffs and be linked together.

The challenge is for each team of two people to become disconnected from their partners, without removing their handcuffs from their wrists and without untying the knots. The challenge is complete when everyone in the group is disconnected from his or her partner.

Initially, many groups attempt a physical solution by stepping over their partner's handcuffs and other various movements. They will find out soon enough that this does not lead to a solution. Encourage them to keep track of what works and what doesn't and to try new things. For example, if they are facing each other (they usually are), have them stand side by side. Does this change the way they would define the problem?

After about five minutes, call a time-out and ask them to define the problem they are trying to solve. You will hear something like, "We are trying to get disconnected from each other."

Validate their problem statements and ask, "What are some other ways we could define this challenge?"

As the activity continues, you can increase hints and clues by asking them to narrow their focus to the loops surrounding their wrists. The phrase "look for a window of opportunity," can be helpful. In this case, the window of opportunity is the loop at the end of each rope handcuff. Listen for someone to say, "I need to get my rope around my partner's hand or arm." Jump on comments like this! Ask how they could rephrase their problem to reflect this aspect of the challenge.

By sliding your rope under the loop of your partner's handcuffs and then over his or her hand, you can solve this puzzle. It's a good idea to practice this activity before doing it with your group so you can demonstrate the solution.

Discussion Questions

1. What were your mental handcuffs?
2. What does this tell us about problem solving?
3. What assumptions did you make?
4. What phantom rules did you adhere to?
5. What happened when you changed your perspective?
6. How important is it to have a well-defined problem?

Out with the Old

OBJECTIVES
• To use the SCAMPER technique during brainstorming

Group Size
Up to 10

Materials
Large-size sticky notes, pens, copies of the
SCAMPER method handout

Time
20 to 30 minutes

Procedure

Send out a statement of the brainstorming topic
ahead of time to all group members. Give them
a premeeting homework assignment: Everyone
has to come to the meeting with one idea written on a large-size sticky note. As they arrive at
the brainstorming session, have them put their ideas up on the wall for all
to see. Remind everyone of the topic, then go through each idea one by one,
allowing all team members to read and clarify (and rewrite if necessary)
their idea.

Now you are ready to start brainstorming. Challenge the group to come
up with something different from any idea currently posted on the wall.
They are not allowed to use any existing idea the way it is—that is, they
can combine ideas, manipulate them, change them, or rearrange them, but
they cannot use any single idea anyone brought.

Give everyone a copy of the SCAMPER method handout for the team
to refer to. Encourage them to use as many of the strategies as they can to
change, combine, and alter the original ideas to create something new.

The seven strategies of the SCAMPER method are:

1. **S**ubstitute—components, materials, people

2. **C**ombine—join two or more elements.

3. **A**dapt—change some part of the problem so it works where it didn't before. Change the function.

4. **M**odify—make it bigger or smaller; change the shape, color, or other attributes.

5. **P**urpose—modify the purpose; put to another use. Think about what it's supposed to do or what it's typically used for and challenge any assumptions.

6. **E**liminate—simplify, remove any or all elements; reduce to core functionality.

7. **R**everse—make it go upside down, inside out, or in reverse. Make it go in the opposite direction from the one that was originally intended.

Change 5 or 10

OBJECTIVES
- To practice the SCAMPER technique
- To experience the ebb and flow natural to creativity and brainstorming

Group Size

Any

Materials

Copies of the SCAMPER method handouts (p. 76) posted in the room

Time

10 to 15 minutes

Procedure

"Change 3" is a popular icebreaker often used to demonstrate our reactions to change. This version takes the Change 3 idea to the extreme. We like it because it forces teams to go beyond the obvious to generate solutions.

To play, pair up group members and have them face each other. (If you have an odd number in your group, assign one person the role of observer.) Give the pairs about 45 seconds to look at each other. After time is up, have pairs stand back-to-back to each another.

Each person is then going to change two things about their appearance. Give the group 30 seconds to do this. Then ask players to stand face-to-face with their partner and try to discover the changes that they made in their appearance. Each person takes a turn to point out the two changes made by his or her partner. Another 45 seconds should be enough time for this.

After this exchange, have partners go back-to-back again and have each person change three more things about his or her appearance (we are now at five changes total). After 45 seconds have the partners turn to face each other and see if each partner can spot the three new changes. After this exchange, partners go back-to-back again for four more changes, then face-to-face to see if they can spot them.

Then it's back-to-back again for six more changes (we're now at 15 total!). At this point, you might notice groans or other reactions from the group regarding this request. This is the perfect time to remind the team of the SCAMPER method and ask them what they can do that they have not yet tried. See if they can consider ways to deal with the challenge differently. Give them about a minute for this round. Partners then go face-to-face once more to discover changes.

The first SCAMPER strategy you observe will be Eliminate. People will take off jewelry, watches, or shoes. Most people don't look beyond themselves as they attempt to change their appearance. Once you mention the SCAMPER method, you will see some people get excited with the new possibilities! Could someone pick up an object from the room that would change his or her appearance (adding or combining to with what that person already has)? What if two people exchanged partners (Substituting)? How many changes would that be?

Discussion Questions

1. What possibilities did SCAMPER open you to? Can you give some examples?
2. How did forcing the number of changes you had to make influence your thinking?
3. In what ways are these methods helpful during brainstorming?

1, 2, 3

OBJECTIVES
- To understand how time constraints can assist in the brainstorming process
- To experience a shift in thinking

Group Size

Any

Materials

One blank sheet of paper for each person

Time

10 minutes

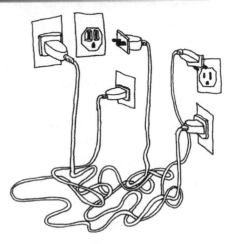

Procedure

To start, have the group gather around you with some open space in the center. Hand everyone a sheet of paper and ask them to place it on the ground in the center space. Invite them to use all the space; the paper should not be stacked or touching another sheet.

Tell the group that the sheets of paper and the people in the group are the only resources they can use during the activity. Give them the safety parameters: pushing, pulling, or lifting. And no interfering with any changes the facilitator makes during the game (that's you!).

For this game, wording is key, so please use this exact wording. Tell the group:

"After giving you about 30 seconds to develop and discuss your plan I will count to 3. For example: 1, 2, 3 (demonstrating this may get a few laughs). On the count of 3, no one in the group should be touching the ground. When I say 'done' you can relax; that round will be considered over."

After that round (and each subsequent round), ask the group how successful they think they were. Before the next round, gather up a few of their sheets of paper and eliminate them from the activity. The directions are the same for the second round (once again, follow the exact wording described above). Again, you as the facilitator will remove a few more sheets of paper before the start of a new round. Be sure to give the group a few minutes between rounds to brainstorm ways to achieve success.

What will it take for the group to continue to succeed with this challenge?

Sharing what's left of the paper (by tearing it into smaller pieces) is an obvious solution to be "off the ground." However, when you eliminate most, or all, of the paper, another solution must be considered.

Possible paradigm shift: The words "On the count of 3, no one in the group should be touching the ground" can take on another meaning. If the group gets to the point when there are few options left, repeat the instructions, exaggerating the part where you say "touching the ground." And then start the count immediately and very slowly so they can adjust on the fly if somebody figures it out.

If the group coordinates themselves to jump off the ground so no one in the group is touching the ground when you say "3," would this not be a solution?

Discussion Questions

1. Did you feel pressured or forced by the time constraints? What effect did this have on the outcome?

2. Were all ideas heard? Why or why not?

3. What plan took shape?

4. Did your plan change along the way?

5. What did it take for your group to figure it out? In what ways would it benefit us to change our way of thinking as we did in this game?

6. How does this relate to brainstorming?

Cross Over

OBJECTIVES
- To actively engage in brainstorming as a team
- To challenge group members to think outside the box

Group Size

6 to 20 people. An even number is required for this game. If you have an odd number of people, assign someone the role of observer.

Materials

Large paper plate, stopwatch

Time

15 to 20 minutes

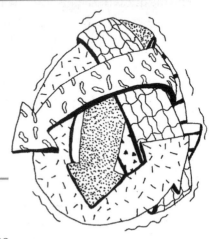

Procedure

Cross Over is an active thinking game that will get people up and moving. Place the paper plate on the ground and have everyone form a large circle around it. Make sure the group is evenly spaced around the paper plate. Ask the group members to point to the person directly across from them in the circle. That is their partner. Once everyone is in place, give them the goal and the rules, using the script provided below. It's important to follow the script exactly, because the wording is intended to open up possibilities.

"Your challenge is to touch the paper plate and switch places with your partner as quickly as you can, without touching anyone else at any time. I will start the clock when someone yells 'go' and I will stop the clock when everybody has switched places and somebody yells 'stop.' If anyone violates the rules by touching someone else, I will add one second per infraction."

After their first attempt, ask the group how they can do it in half the time. Give them an opportunity to brainstorm and practice to see if they can meet the new time goal.

Once they meet the new time goal, continue challenging them to cut their goal in half until they get to a point where they can complete the challenge in under two to ten seconds, depending on the size of the group. To do it this quickly, the group may need to think in entirely new ways.

As the group is working through the challenge, they may ask questions to clarify the rules. Every question gets answered by restating the script above.

The group may come up with a variety of time-cutting ideas, such as: stand closer, stand next to their partner, move the paper plate, or even cut up the paper plate. All ideas are allowed, as long as the original rules are adhered to.

Tips

This is a great activity for newly formed teams. It gets participants to consider different perspectives, to listen, and to be open to others' ideas.

Because these are the very skills that contribute to effective brainstorming, it is beneficial for the team to practice and build upon these types of skills early on.

Discussion Questions

1. What skills or characteristics did you have to tap into to discover additional solutions?
2. Were all ideas heard? Why or why not?
3. Do you usually take the time to discover additional solutions once you have made up your mind?
4. How difficult was it to come up with the fastest solution? In what ways did you have to alter your thinking?
5. How can we apply these skills to generating ideas in a brainstorming session?

6

It's a Storm, Not a Drizzle

The best way to get a good idea is to get a lot of ideas.

—Linus Pauling

Bad Ideas Welcome! Part 2

OBJECTIVES
- To use bad ideas to help the group uncover great ideas
- To clarify which features or elements of your topic should be avoided or eliminated

Group Size

Any

Materials

Pen and paper, or markers and flip chart

Time

15 to 25 minutes

Procedure

Sometimes knowing what you don't want helps you clarify what you do want. In this fun and revealing exercise, turn your brainstorming topic on its head by coming up with a list of features or qualities that will make it worse. Once you've generated a bunch of "bad" ideas, you will be able to look to their opposites for ideas about how to make your actual brainstorming subject better.

Start by having the group rephrase their original brainstorming topic, this time stating it in opposite terms. For example, "Let's brainstorm ways to attract more customers to our Grand Opening" could be restated as, "Let's brainstorm ways to convince nobody to attend our Grand Opening."

Once the topic has been restated, let the group brainstorm a list of bad, outrageous, and truly ridiculous ideas. Make it fun for everyone by starting with some terrible ideas of your own. Using our Grand Opening example, here are some suggestions to ensure that no one will attend:

- Hold the event during a snowstorm.
- Make sure the parking lot can only accommodate four cars.

- Don't advertise it, or advertise it with a tiny ad in a newspaper nobody reads.
- Feature lousy has-been entertainers to bore the crowd.
- Don't provide any special perks for attendees.
- Hold the event on Super Bowl Sunday.

For your bad-idea brainstorming session, follow the same rules as you would in a normal session. Encourage members to generate as many ideas as possible, combine and build on one another's bad ideas, and go for wildly exaggerated ideas. Allow enough time to generate a solid list of ideas. Remind group members that although the activity is fun, there's a purpose behind it. Keep the discussion moving and don't allow the novelty of the exercise to cause you to cut it short.

After the group has generated their list of bad ideas, spend some time discussing why the ideas are bad. This will help the group clarify features or elements that should be avoided or eliminated.

Have them think about the opposites of their bad ideas. Doing this can give your group clues pointing to what might be good ideas. For instance, the opposite of "Hold the event on Super Bowl Sunday" from our Grand Opening example might be "Schedule the event on a day when there's absolutely nothing important going on." The opposite of "Feature lousy has-been entertainers to bore the crowd" would be "Get Bieber on the phone!"

This exercise is not only fun but can reveal some valuable lessons for the group.

Lead-in Activity

To get your group's bad ideas flowing, try starting with the activity called Bad Ideas Welcome! Part 1 on page 43. This lead-in activity lets people generate a rapid-fire list of truly terrible ideas about a fun topic unrelated to their real-life challenge. It's a great way to prime the pump before diving into your group's "real" issue.

Discussion Questions

1. Was it easy to generate a list of bad ideas? Why or why not?

2. In what ways do bad ideas lead to good ideas?

3. How can we make sure we encourage all ideas when we brainstorm?

4. Why is it sometimes difficult for individuals to let go of ideas?

SCAMPER Sculptures

OBJECTIVES
- To brainstorm together on a fun and creative building challenge
- To get to know the strategies of the SCAMPER brainstorming method

Group Size

Any, split into small teams of 3 to 4

Materials

One handout describing the strategies of the SCAMPER method per team (provided on page 76), plus an assortment of props and materials. Here are some suggestions: balloons, drinking straws, pipe cleaners, craft sticks (popsicle sticks), rubber bands, paper clips, index cards, spoons, forks, plastic cups, sheets of paper, a roll of tape, marshmallows, Play-Doh, cardboard sleeve from a coffee cup, toothpicks, rulers, pencils, etc. Add fun items at will!

Time

30 to 35 minutes

Procedure

This enjoyable, freestyle building challenge gives group members an opportunity to brainstorm together while experiencing the SCAMPER method in action.

Split the group into small teams of three to four people each. Each team is responsible for creating a modern art–style sculpture using the materials provided. Encourage them to be as creative as possible. Don't limit teams to using just the items provided. If they want to bring in some outside materials, that's okay.

Each team's sculpture must meet the following criteria:

- Must be at least 1½ feet tall
- Must use at least 15 different items
- Must be able to stand on its own, without external support

And most importantly,

- At least seven of the items in their sculpture must be connected to each other based on each of the seven SCAMPER strategies.

To do this, teams will need to think about each of the strategies of the SCAMPER method, and figure out how to build that strategy into their sculpture. Here are some examples:

- The "S" in SCAMPER stands for Substitute. A team might decide to use a marshmallow as a substitute for glue to hold some parts together.
- The "M" in SCAMPER stands for Modify. A team could decide to modify a sheet of paper by rolling it into a tube and standing it on end like a column to support some weight.

Give teams about 25 minutes to create their sculptures or more time if necessary. Once all the teams' SCAMPER sculptures are completed, have each team share their work of art with the rest of the group. Be sure to have each team point out some of their creative interpretations of the SCAMPER strategies.

To learn more about the SCAMPER method, see Chapter 1, "The Weather Forecast Calls for Brainstorming."

In What Ways?

OBJECTIVES
- To clearly define your brainstorming topic
- To stimulate creative thinking

Group Size
Individual, or groups of up to 12

Materials
In What Ways? handout

Time
10 to 20 minutes

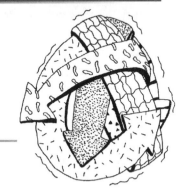

Procedure

Prior to the start of your session, it's important to provide the group with a statement of the problem or topic they will be brainstorming about. Announcing the topic of the brainstorming session in advance allows individuals time to mull over the topic, let it sink in, and come up with some ideas before the meeting begins. Here is a structured way to ensure you have clearly defined the problem and to give group members the chance to get a head start in generating ideas.

A day or two before your brainstorming session, send an email to everyone in the group stating the problem or goal, along with an attached copy of the In What Ways? handout. Ask team members to set aside at least ten minutes to complete the handout. Have everyone bring their completed handouts to the session.

Begin the brainstorming session with the problem definition you had sent out in advance to the group. Be open to redefining the problem based on the feedback of the group. Once the group has come to a mutually agreed-upon definition, start the brainstorming session using the ideas generated by the group members on their In What Ways? handouts.

Variations

You can also use this technique to generate ideas for individual brainstorming.

In What Ways?

List a challenge you face or will be facing. State it as an idea-finding question. Then restate it several times, trying to get to the broadest possible interpretation.

Challenge: In what ways might we _____

_____

_____

Restatement 1: In what ways might we _____

_____

_____

Restatement 2: In what ways might we _____

_____

_____

Restatement 3: In what ways might we _____

_____

_____

Restatement 4: In what ways might we _____

_____

_____

Restatement 5: In what ways might we _____

_____

_____

HANDOUT

Write your best definition from the previous page. Then list several means (ideas) to meet the challenge.

Challenge: In what ways might we ______________________________

Means (ideas): ______________________________

The World's Greatest Bathtub

OBJECTIVES
- To understand the benefits of generating lots of ideas
- To experience what happens when all the obvious ideas have been exhausted

Group Size

Any, split into teams of 4 to 6

Materials

Flip chart and markers

Time

20 minutes

Procedure

Sometimes groups underestimate their ability to generate a large quantity of ideas. Use this game to illustrate that when we push our team and ourselves, we can come up with far more ideas than we may think possible.

To begin, you will need to split large groups into smaller teams of four to six participants. Give each team a piece of flip-chart paper and a marker. Have each team choose someone to play the role of team scribe. He or she is responsible for writing down all the ideas generated by the team.

Present the brainstorming challenge to the team: They are tasked with creating the World's Greatest Bathtub. Tell them they have four minutes to come up with all the features that would be included in their bathtub. After four minutes, announce that time is up, and ask the scribe to draw a line under the last ideas on their list.

Give the team two more minutes to come up with more qualities for the World's Greatest Bathtub. Announce that time is up after the two minutes have elapsed, and ask the scribe to draw a line under the last of the new ideas.

Tell the team they have another minute to add even more ideas to their list of what to include in the World's Greatest Bathtub. Announce that time is up after the minute has passed, and make sure the scribe add a line under the last of the new items on the list.

Finally, give them one last minute to come up with a final batch of ideas. Be prepared for groans and complaints, but motivate them to push through to see where it takes them. Announce that time is up after one minute, then congratulate the group for a job well done.

Finish by having the group discuss and debrief the experience, using the list of questions provided below. During the discussion, ask group members to think about both the quantity of ideas generated and the quality of ideas generated. Which time block yielded the most ideas, and which block yielded their favorite or "best" ideas?

Discussion Questions

1. Did your team hit the wall during any of the blocks of brainstorming time? What happened after that?

2. Take a look at your lists and choose your most creative ideas. In which block of time did they occur?

3. How did having extra blocks of time after you thought you were done affect your creative output?

4. The brainstorming topic in this exercise (The World's Greatest Bathtub) was intentionally lighthearted. What effect did that have on the process and results? Even if your future topics are of a more serious nature, are there ways to maintain a lighthearted tone?

Magic Wand

OBJECTIVES
- To remove constraints that thwart creativity
- To generate a fun way to combat negative feedback

Group Size
Any
Materials
None
Time
No extra time necessary

Procedure

The Magic Wand is a fun and useful tool to help groups or individuals cast off limiting beliefs and free them to dream up creative solutions during the brainstorming process.

It is sometimes tempting for groups, especially those with a firmly established work culture, to immediately brush aside certain ideas during brainstorming that "just don't fit" within the parameters, norms, or guidelines of their workplace. Tell the group that they have been given an imaginary Magic Wand that anyone can use at any time to vanquish those limiting "that just doesn't fit" statements with a wave of the wand!

As facilitator, use the Magic Wand if you detect that one of the parameters, norms, or limiting beliefs of their workplace is causing the team to be stuck. A good indicator of a rule to "wave away" is when you overhear someone say, "That won't work here," or "We tried that before, and it didn't work." Quickly assess what rule is holding them back and use your Magic Wand to wave it away for a few minutes.

Team members can also get into the spirit, using the Magic Wand privilege any time. It's rewarding to see group members grasp the idea. When someone shoots down one of their brainstorming suggestions, they can respond, "Hey, I was using the Magic Wand—of course it will work!" Providing the group with a Magic Wand helps keep the tone light and gives participants a handy tool for dealing with the negative comments or limiting beliefs that can undermine the brainstorming process.

Tips

Use some sort of prop for your Magic Wand. It can be a drinking straw, a ruler, a stick, a pen . . . get creative and have fun with it!

Discussion Questions

1. What are some of the benefits of having a Magic Wand?

2. What are some limiting beliefs that hold back your team or organization?

3. Which of those limiting beliefs would you most want to vanquish with your Magic Wand? Why?

4. In what ways do negative comments affect people's level of participation?

Plan B

OBJECTIVES
- To practice refraining from judgment of ideas
- To expand the number of ideas generated by the group
- To improve team members' ability to let go of ideas they've become attached to

Group Size

Individual, or groups of 4 to 7

Materials

Paper and pens

Time

10 to 15 minutes

Procedure

At the start of your session, after posing the brainstorming problem or topic, let the team know that you are not looking for the best ideas, but rather their second best, or Plan B, ideas. Approach this as you would a "normal" brainstorming session, allowing about ten minutes for the group to generate all the Plan B ideas they can think of.

Most groups find it challenging to come up with a list of Plan B ideas. They become attached to their original ideas and are reluctant to let them go.

After they've created their list of Plan B ideas, it may be worthwhile for the group to take a few minutes to consider and discuss some of the questions that follow.

Variations

You can also use this perspective to generate more ideas when a team is stuck with a current solution and have reached a dead end with the idea.

Tips

If someone comes up with a really good idea, note it but consider saying, "That idea is too good." See if it catches on. This is a good technique to use if you plan to follow with the discussion questions.

Discussion Questions

1. What made this so challenging?
2. How did this assignment change your thinking?
3. Were all ideas heard? Why or why not?
4. Did anyone hear that his or her ideas were too good to be a Plan B idea? How did it feel to hear this? How was it different than hearing "that won't work, because . . ."?

Disregardables

OBJECTIVES

- To understand the difference between real and perceived obstacles
- To experience how constraints can lead to creativity

Group Size

Any

Materials

Rules and Regulations for Use handout

Time

20 to 40 minutes

Procedure

Some of the best ideas never see the light in a brainstorming session because we tend to self-edit before we utter a word. We come up with all sorts of reasons to discount our ideas. Even though it's a well-known technique to take away all the rules, or to play the "what if?" card, we still like to invent rules that create obstacles for brainstorming. This game takes the opposite approach to help build creativity, generate ideas, and perhaps demonstrate the role that rules play when it comes to brainstorming. The idea is to start with a cumbersome rule or obstacle and see how creative the group can be within the limitations imposed by the rule.

Pre-assignment: Have each person bring three rules or guidelines taken from commonly used products. For example, you may be familiar with this guideline found on most toasters: "Do not immerse in water and unplug before cleaning." Give your group a couple of examples to get them on the right track. Having everyone bring rules will give you a nice supply to use when you think the group is stuck, to generate creative thinking, or to just have some fun. Even without doing the prework, we have you covered. The

Rules and Regulations for Use handout provides a long list of "disregard-ables" to choose from.

How to use: Apply the rule to your group's situation to see where it leads the discussion and what ideas it generates.

Look at the reason or benefit of the rule. How does it help? Why was it created? How is it implemented? How is it regulated?

Just like the concept of using word prompts to assist creativity, you only get one rule to use, so as facilitator make the team stick with the rule until you think all possibilities have been discussed.

Tips

Use our list the first time to give the team the idea, and then ask them to bring in some of their own rules. Using their rules gives a sense of owner-ship to the process and makes it more personal. People get really proud of their rules. Be sure to keep these rules for future brainstorming sessions.

Rules and Regulations for Use

1. You have to be four feet tall to go on this ride
2. Don't immerse in water
3. Dry clean only
4. Do not turn upside down
5. May be harmful if swallowed
6. No stopping or standing
7. One size fits all
8. Shake well
9. For a limited time only
10. Do not remove tag under penalty of law
11. Please don't feed the animals
12. May cause drowsiness
13. Keep out of reach of children
14. Do not use near fire, flame, or sparks
15. Objects in mirror may appear smaller than they are
16. Fragile. Do not drop.
17. May contain small parts
18. For use by trained personnel only
19. For outdoor use only
20. No purchase necessary
21. Safe for use around pets
22. Not to be used as a personal flotation device
23. The timer can be set up to seven days in advance
24. Different bait is used to catch different fish
25. All dogs must be on a leash
26. Refrigerate after opening
27. Slippery when wet
28. Do not operate under the influence
29. Not intended for highway use

Grab and Go Brainstorming Tips: Ten Ways to Capture Your Great Ideas

We've all experienced it. The brilliant idea that comes when you least expect it. Maybe it hits you while you're out grocery shopping or taking the dogs for a walk. Or maybe while you're in the shower or taking the kids to soccer practice. How many times have we told ourselves, "Don't let me forget that one!" And poof! Away it goes just a few minutes later, replaced by other more urgent thoughts.

When good ideas come, don't leave remembering them to chance. Be prepared to capture them. Here are some suggestions to keep your best ideas from slipping away:

1. Carry a pocket-sized notepad and pen with you at all times. A spiral notebook is good, but because you'll be using it often, you may want to upgrade to a better-quality notebook like a Moleskine or Rhodia product.

2. Download and use a good note-taking app on your smartphone or mobile device. One of our favorites is Evernote (www.evernote.com). This top-rated app syncs across a wide variety of devices including iPhones, Android phones, iPads and BlackBerry products, as well as your PC or Mac computer.

3. Keep a sketch pad or notepad on your nightstand.

4. Leave a voicemail for yourself on your home or office answering machine.

5. Email your idea to yourself.

6. Share your idea with a friend, colleague, or family member. Be sure the person you share it with is positive, nonjudgmental, and trustworthy.

7. Text your good idea to yourself.

8. Repeat it to yourself out loud. If you don't have access to pen and paper, a smartphone, computer, or other recording device, speak the idea out loud to yourself a few times.

9. If your best ideas happen in the shower, jot them in a waterproof notepad. You'll find all-weather writing pads and pencils online or at most outdoor recreation or camping supply stores. You may also prefer an underwater dive slate, available at scuba supply stores.

10. Record your great ideas using a built-in voice recording app on your smart-phone, or with a lightweight digital voice recorder.

7

"Yes! and . . ."

If I have seen further it is by standing on the shoulders of giants.

—Isaac Newton

Alphabet Improv

OBJECTIVE
- To build creativity

Group Size

Any, split into teams of 3 or 4

Materials

Stopwatch

Time

10 to 15 minutes

Procedure

Improvisation performance, or improv, is acting, singing, talking, or creating comedy in the moment. It usually involves starting with an idea from the audience or a prompt from a fellow performer. Improv is a highly creative and intuitive art that one can become better at with lots of practice. It uses the skills of listening, thinking, and building on one another's ideas. Improv embodies the concept of "Yes! and . . ."

In improv it's all about setting the other person up for success, which is also an important part of brainstorming. To be able to do this, listening is the key. It's okay to pause and consider what you will say next. You are always building on what the other person comes up with. This game is a fun way to practice these helpful skills.

Have the group split into smaller teams of three people. If you have additional people, a couple of teams consisting of four team members is acceptable. Have one person from each team shout out a random topic and another person from the team yell out a letter of the alphabet. Tell the teams to keep these two "prompts" in mind—their topic and the letter of the alphabet.

Tell the teams that they have 90 seconds to get through the alphabet, starting with their chosen letter, continuing through the alphabet as far as they can go before time runs out. They need to construct a sentence, one person and one word at a time, that pertains to their topic. To do this, each person will add a word to the sentence using the next letter of the alphabet.

For example:

Topic: Books, and the letter *G*

G   Good
H   History
I   Is
J   Just
K   Knowing
L   Legendary
M   Men
N   Not
O   Ordinary
P   People
Q   Quite
R   Realistically

If they get to the letter *Z* and there is time left, they can continue back to the letter *A* and see if they can get all the way around to where they started.

Does it always make sense? No! Is that okay? Yes! As you can see from the example, their sentence may or may not make sense grammatically or logically, but that's okay! The point is to think in the moment, listen to each other, and build on one another's ideas. Now that they have the hang of it, go for a second round. This time teams switch topics and letters or come up with new ones, so no one gets too easy an idea.

Discussion Questions

1. What impact did the 90-second deadline have on creativity?

2. What impact did it have on how judgmental you were about each other's ideas?

3. Did you find you were more or less accepting of ideas under such a time crunch?

4. How do games like this help build our creative muscle?

Team Machine

Group Size

Up to 20 people

Materials

None

Time

10 minutes

Procedure

This is an improv-type game that starts with the group in a circle. One person goes into the middle of the circle and acts out one component of a machine, complete with movement and sound effects. Then another person adds his or her component to the machine—integrating this new "part" of the machine with that of the person who came before. For example, person one hits one fist with the other, swings an arm out and hits his or her fist again, making a sound effect. Person two puts his or her knee beside the first person's fist and steps up and down every time the fist gets hit and jars the knee. Their "parts" must stay in motion until the entire "machine" is up and running and everyone has added their component to the machine. When everyone has joined the machine, give it about ten seconds to "run" and make a corny comment such as, "I always knew we were a well-oiled machine." Let the groans ensue!

Discussion Question

1. How do we apply the spirit of "adding on" in our brainstorming sessions?

Zap Negativity

OBJECTIVES
- To keep negative members from derailing your brainstorming session
- To give the group control over their actions and responses

Group Size

Any, split into teams of 3 or 4

Materials

One copy of Zap Negativity handout

Time

10 minutes

Procedure

Even the most positive team members can be unaware of how easily negative comments and feedback can creep into a brainstorming session. This activity will help your group build an awareness of negativity, and also give group members control over their actions and reactions. Split the group into smaller teams of three or four people. Give each team a copy of the Zap Negativity handout and allow six minutes for them to come up with their best counter-comments for each of the negative comments listed. Bring the small teams back together to share ideas and discuss with the whole group. Follow up with your brainstorming session and see what a difference it makes!

Zap Negativity

What is the best way to counter these negative comments and nonverbal messages?

- "I totally disagree."
- "But what about . . ."
- "Yeah, but . . ."
- Roll your eyes.
- Sigh.
- Lean back in your chair.
- Cross your arms.
- Keep checking your phone or watch.
- "This is a dumb topic."
- "This is a waste of time."
- "I don't even know why we're doing this."
- "I think we get the point of this activity."
- "Seriously?" or "You can't be serious!"
- "Realistically, how is that possible?"
- "I don't think there is anything else we can add to this."
- "I think we're good."
- "Let's move on."

Beginnings and Endings

OBJECTIVES
- To practice listening skills
- To experience building on each other's ideas

Group Size

Up to 20, split into two teams

Materials

None

Time

10 minutes

Procedure

Divide your group into two teams. Each team will get the other team started. Have each team start by calling out a kickoff word (no proper names or capitalized words allowed) to the other team. It adds to the fun if the kickoff words are vivid or creative. Once a team receives its kickoff word from the other team, the goal is to come up with a new word that starts with the last letter of the kickoff word.

Example: car, restaurant, turnpike, elephant, trapeze, eel, lightning, gift, and so on.

Here are the rules:

- Once a team receives the kickoff word, anyone on the team can add a new word.
- Team members must then take turns adding words. No one may go twice in a row.
- All new words must be added within two seconds.
- If someone takes more than two seconds to add a word, the team loses the round and must start again.

The team that can continuously come up with a word that fits the most times wins.

Have a friendly competition to see which team can go the longest. Play a couple of rounds if time allows. Team members may become so good at it, you will have to call time after five minutes of play!

Discussion Questions

1. How did this game challenge your team?

2. Did your team develop any strategies to become better?

3. What does this activity tell us about the brainstorming process?

No Way, Yes Way

OBJECTIVES
- To experience the impact of feedback during brainstorming
- To discover how to encourage creative thinking

Group Size

Up to 16, split into two teams

Materials

Negative Team Member's Script and Positive Team Member's Script handouts

Time

15 to 20 minutes

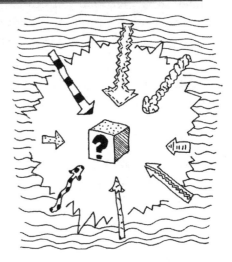

Procedure

This activity gives group members a chance to experience the impact a positive person can have on a group versus the impact a negative person can have on a group. It requires a bit of preparation prior to the meeting. Before the brainstorming session, secretly select one member from each team to assist by agreeing to play specific roles during the meeting. One person will play the role of the negative naysayer; one will play the role of an encourager. Provide each person with the appropriate script to study beforehand.

At the beginning of your meeting, say to the group, "Before we get into our actual brainstorm, let's take 15 minutes to get our creative juices flowing. We will do that by brainstorming about a fun and unrelated topic. To make this manageable, let's split the group into two smaller teams. You have seven minutes to brainstorm 50 ideas to make the world's coolest pogo stick. Ready, go!" (Make sure the negative naysayer and the encourager are each on a different team).

After seven minutes, get the teams' attention. Thank them for taking the time to generate ideas on the topic, and say to everyone:

"In a moment I'd like both teams to share some of the great ideas you came up with. But first, it's time for me to come clean. Before we started, I assigned some secret and specific roles for a couple of your teammates. [At this point, acknowledge the actors and thank them for their "Oscar-worthy" acting skills.] Team A, you may have noticed a negative person in your midst, while Team B, you probably felt some very encouraging and positive energy from one of your team members. Let's talk about how that affected your discussion."

Allow five to ten minutes for discussion, using the questions below. After the discussion, give both teams a chance to share some of their best and most creative pogo stick ideas!

Discussion Questions

1. What was the tone of your discussion? What contributed to the overall tone you experienced?
2. Team A, you had a negative person; did you feel shut down? What was that like? Were you more or less likely to contribute after that happened? How did that divert your attention from the topic at hand?
3. Team B, you were supported and encouraged in a very positive way; how would you describe that experience? Did that impact the number of ideas you generated? What other benefits came from the positive feedback?
4. Now that we are ready to brainstorm our issue, what are some ways we can encourage the creativity of our team and generate the most ideas?

Negative Team Member's Script

Your job is to play a negative role in the team's conversation. During brainstorming time, you will need to subvert the process or shoot down ideas as they are brought up. Please try to do this in a subtle way so the team does not catch on that you were assigned this role. If you are naturally a positive person, you will have to work extra hard so that the group does not discover that you are a "plant." Here are some suggested phrases or actions that you can say or do that will create a negative tone.

- "I totally disagree."
- "But what about . . ."
- "Yeah, but . . ."
- Roll your eyes.
- Sigh.
- Lean back in your chair.
- Cross your arms.
- Keep checking your phone or watch.
- "This is a ridiculous topic."
- "This is a waste of time."
- "I don't even know why we're doing this."
- "I think we get the point of this activity."
- "Seriously?" or "You can't be serious!"
- "Realistically, how is that possible?"
- "I don't think there is anything else we can add to this."
- "I think we're good."
- "Let's move on."

Positive Team Member's Script

Your job is to play a positive role in the team's conversation. During brainstorming time, you will need to energize the process by uplifting and encouraging your teammates. Please try to do this in a subtle way so the team does not catch on that you were assigned this role. You may have to work extra hard to come across as sincere, rather than patronizing, so that the group does not discover that you are a "plant." Here are some suggested phrases or actions that you can say or do that will create a positive tone.

- "Tell me more about that idea."
- "Keep going."
- "Great idea! Who can add to that?"
- "These are all great ideas, what else?"
- "I love it!"
- "You always come up with good ideas."
- "We should work for Mattel."
- "I wish I had that in my pogo stick."
- "I would pay for that feature."
- "My kids would love that!"
- Nod.
- Smile.
- Make eye contact.
- Lean forward in your chair.
- "We can do this!"

Garage Band

OBJECTIVES
- To build creative thinking on the team
- To experience collaboration and a sense of flow

Group Size

Any, working in teams of 5

Materials

Assorted items listed below

Time

25 to 30 minutes

Procedure

This activity is lots of fun and guaranteed to stretch people's comfort zones in new directions!

In his book *Group Genius,* Keith Sawyer talks about the idea of "flow" and how he has experienced flow when playing in his jazz band or on the basketball court. To achieve flow, team members need to practice spending more time observing and listening to others and less time planning their own responses. This activity is a way for team members to practice listening, observing, and collaborating. If they are lucky, they may even get to experience "flow."

Place several common items on a table. Examples of the items are:

- Soda cans
- Combs
- Water bottles
- Coffee cups
- Computer keyboard
- Keys
- Box of paper clips

Split the group into teams of five people each. Tell all participants they can choose any item from the table (each person gets one item), or if you are in a place where other items are readily available, invite them to find one of their own. Whichever item they choose will become their musical instrument.

Tell participants that every team has now been magically transformed into a garage band, known for its wild creativity and amazing musical prowess. Teams have 20 minutes to:

- Name their band.
- Create a song, beat, chant, or invent another type of musical number that incorporates the sounds of each of their musical instruments.
- Practice or rehearse their song.

Remind teams to have fun and ham it up, but try to take the musical part seriously. See if they can come up with something that combines all their sounds and gives everyone a chance to play in sync together.

At the end of 20 minutes, invite each garage band to perform their song for the rest of the group. Encourage audience members to cheer, whistle, and applaud wildly for each of the teams.

Tips
If you have any real musicians on your team, spread them out so that each team has some natural musical talent.

Discussion Questions
1. How did you feel when it was time to perform? Nervous? Energized? Self-conscious? Ready to rock? Why?
2. What enhances individual and team creativity?
3. What are obstacles to creativity?
4. Did you get into the flow as you were creating music?
5. If so, what was that like? What contributed to the feeling of flow?
6. How can we achieve flow in our brainstorming sessions?

Feedback About Feedback

OBJECTIVES
- To discover feedback styles of the brainstorming team
- To create a deeper level of trust among group members

Group Size
Any
Materials
None
Time
10 minutes

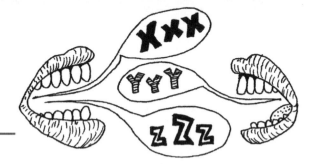

Procedure

Before the brainstorming session, assign each person a partner. During the course of your session, have each person observe the communication and feedback style of his or her partner. Tell each one to take a few mental notes that they will later share with his or her partner. Things to watch for could include:

- Did he or she actively offer feedback during the session?
- What kind of feedback did he or she provide?
- Did he or she "say" anything with nonverbal communication?
- Did he or she offer any type of encouraging statements?
- Did he or she ask helpful questions?

After the brainstorming session, have each pair discuss their findings. After the partner discussions, follow up with a group conversation about feedback, and how it can contribute to or derail the brainstorming process. Use the discussion questions that follow, or ask some questions of your own.

Discussion Questions

1. What are some feedback methods we use during brainstorming?

2. How does our feedback help or hinder the process?

3. What types of feedback promote idea contribution?

4. What can you do differently, based on what your partner observed?

Doodle Round, Doodle Sound

OBJECTIVES
• To add to the ideas of others
• To experience collaboration

Group Size

Any, split into teams of 5 to 7

Materials

Paper and markers

Time

10 to 15 minutes

Procedure

Play this fun game in three rounds. Round one is played without background music; round two is played with classical music in the background; and round three is played with techno, rock and roll, or disco music in the background.

Ask one person on each team to act as his or her team leader for round one. The leader's role is to start a drawing with one or two simple shapes, lines, or squiggles. When he or she is finished, the paper is passed to the person on the right. For the duration of the game, the leader serves as the pacer and tells the team members when to pass the paper. Ask the leaders to allow between five and ten seconds for each person on his or her team to add to the drawing. The first drawing is complete when it makes one full round and everyone on the team has had a chance to add to it.

Round two and round three are played the same way, this time with the different types of music playing in the background.

After the three rounds are completed, have the teams present their drawings to the large group.

It is fun at this point to see if the teams can guess which drawings were from which round (does the music make a difference?).

No discussion is permitted during the drawing. Discourage team members from deciding what to draw before the rounds begin . . . all drawings and ideas should happen in real time while the round is under way.

Tips
Request that the teams use a different person to lead each round.

Discussion Questions

1. When brainstorming, we often hear of flexibility, keeping an open mind, using a "yes! and . . ." approach, and listening as important qualities. In what ways did we use or see these qualities demonstrated in this game?
2. Leaders, what was your expectation of the completed drawing?
3. Did your expectations change?
4. What was the effect of the different types of music? Did you have a preference?
5. How can we apply these ideas to our brainstorming sessions?

Pass It & Plus It

OBJECTIVES
- To generate a list of ideas based on the input of team members
- To elicit ideas from every group member in the brainstorming process

Group Size

6 to 12

Materials

Pen and paper for each participant

Time

10 to 15 minutes

Procedure

This structured "Yes! and . . ." exercise gives everyone an opportunity to contribute, as group members build on one another's thoughts in order to create lists of great brainstorming ideas.

Give every group member a sheet of paper. Have them write just one thought or idea based on your brainstorming topic. Next, have each group member pass his or her sheet of paper to the person on their right. Instruct them to add a thought or idea to their new page, based on the thought or idea preceding it. Participants can add their ideas in a traditional bullet-list format, or they can record their ideas as a word cloud, writing it anywhere on the page and connecting related ideas with lines.

After all group members have added to their new page, instruct them to again pass it to the person on their right. Continue all the way around the table until each page has circled back to the person who started it.

Remind the group that this is truly a "Yes! and . . ." activity. The goal is to explore how to play off and add to one another's ideas. Therefore, each person's contribution to a page should somehow be connected to one of the ideas preceding it on that page. They should avoid adding ideas that cannot be easily related to what is already on the page.

As the pages are passed around the table, each list will begin to take on a unique character. Be sure to display the lists after all the pages have been passed all the way around the group. You may find it useful to make copies of all the lists and distribute them to everyone in the group.

Once all the lists have been generated, use them as a starting point for the rest of your brainstorming session. As always, group members should be encouraged to add to the lists, combine ideas, and rearrange concepts in lots of different ways.

Variations

In addition to writing words on the pages, group members can sketch, draw, or doodle their ideas using colored markers or crayons.

Grab and Go Brainstorming Tips: Ten Ways to Neutralize Naysayers

In addition to using the following ten responses, encourage participants to be flexible in their thinking and follow a "Yes! and . . ." approach to the exercise.

Negative Phrases or Actions:	Your Response:
• "I totally disagree."	"What is something about the idea you agree with?"
• Sigh	"Do we need a short break to get some fresh air?"
• Cross their arms.	"Is it cold in here?"
• Keep checking their phone or watch.	Enforce the no phone rule. Ask "How are we doing on time?" Based on the answer, either negotiate more time or acknowledge that you are within any time limits.
• "This is a waste of time."	"I think we are making some good progress here."
• "I don't even know why we're doing this."	"Sometimes in brainstorming, the best idea becomes clear after the storm."
• "Realistically, how is that possible?"	"We will take time after we are done brainstorming to figure out how to get it done."
• "There's nothing else we can add to this."	"That's usually when the most creative and innovative ideas come out."
• "I think we're good with this."	"Yes, we are good, let's go for great!"
• "Let's move on."	"How about we give ourselves five more minutes and then we will switch gears?"

8

A Brain Flurry

Imagination is more important than knowledge. For while knowledge defines all we currently know and understand, imagination points to all we might yet discover and create.

—Albert Einstein

Pass the Hoop

OBJECTIVES

- To challenge group members to think creatively and build on each other's ideas
- To highlight the benefits of full participation of group members in the brainstorming process
- To experience how having a challenging goal can affect a group's creative output

Group Size

8 to 16

Materials

One medium to large hula hoop, a stopwatch or timer

Time

20 to 30 minutes

Procedure

Pass the Hoop is an active group problem-solving game that gets everyone involved in the brainstorming process. It's a great way to illustrate how building on one another's ideas can lead to amazing results.

Start by having the group members join hands with the people on their left and right, forming one continuous circuit or loop. (Avoid calling it a circle . . . although that is what it will look like at the beginning.) Two of the people will join hands through the middle of the hula hoop. Have group members pass the hoop all the way around the circuit by flipping or tossing it over the head of the person next to them. Once the hula hoop is flipped over someone's head, that person should let it drop down low enough for him or her to step or shimmy out before passing it along to the next person. Without letting go of hands, the group should continue in this manner until the hoop has been passed all the way around, back to the person who started.

The rules:

- No letting go of hands during an attempt.
- Everyone must pass completely through the hula hoop.
- Outside resources are not allowed. The group may use only themselves and the hula hoop for this game.

After they've completed this once, have the group pass the hoop around again, this time setting a time goal for themselves. Give them a couple of attempts to hit their goal. If their goal is too easy, have them set a harder goal. Between each try, give the group a few minutes to brainstorm and explore ways to improve their results.

After the group has reached (or almost reached) their time goal, challenge them to take it to the next level. Tell them:

"You've done great so far and have achieved (or almost achieved) the goals you set for yourself. Now I'd like to really challenge you with the Ultimate Goal—1½ to 2 seconds per person. For example, the Ultimate Goal for a group of ten people would be 15 to 20 seconds. Achieving the Ultimate Goal will require a true breakthrough in thinking, so you'll need to come up with a new solution that looks different from your current one. You can't just do it the same way, only faster!

"Remember, to achieve the Ultimate Goal, the same basic rules apply. You must stay connected in one continuous circuit, holding hands with the person on your left and right; everyone must go all the way through the hoop; and you may only use yourselves and the hula hoop in your solution."

Facilitator's Notes

Allow the group 10 to 15 minutes to brainstorm and practice as they work toward achieving the Ultimate Goal. During this phase, most groups will try out a number of different methods as they begin to zero in on the solution.

There is a "secret solution," where one or more people hold the hoop in place while the group walks or runs through it. This can be done without anyone letting go of hands. If the group discovers this, great. If not, don't force the issue. Let them enjoy the activity on their own terms.

Discussion Questions

1. What were some of the great ideas that helped your group improve its time?
2. How did having a challenging "Ultimate Goal" affect the group's creative output?
3. Would you have been able to achieve the Ultimate Goal using your original method? Why or why not?
4. Did everyone feel empowered to contribute ideas? Why or why not?
5. How would you describe your group's openness to ideas? Why?
6. How would you rate your team in terms of flexibility and openness to change? Why?
7. What are some ways a group can create a climate that encourages full participation from everyone?

Marshmallow Spaghetti Towers

OBJECTIVES
- To understand what motivates us to be creative
- To experience brainstorming in action

Group Size

Any, split into teams of 3 or 4

Materials

One package of spaghetti, one bag of large marshmallows, one bag of small marshmallows, a roll of adhesive tape, and a ruler or tape measure

Time

30 minutes

Procedure

According to a study conducted by researchers at Stanford University, the most innovative teams spend less time in the planning stage and more time in the executing stage. This activity will have teams jumping into action and planning and refining as they go.

Split your group into smaller work teams of three to four people each. Once the teams are created, distribute the spaghetti and marshmallows to each team. Give each team precisely 30 pieces of spaghetti, ten small marshmallows, six inches of tape, and one large marshmallow.

Tell the team members that they have 15 minutes to build the highest freestanding tower they can that will support the weight of the large marshmallow. Their building supplies consist of just the spaghetti, the tape, and the small marshmallows. The tower must be able to stand on its own without tipping over.

After 15 minutes, call time. Have some fun with the testing phase. Make it a big production. Go around to each structure, building suspense and drama as you measure the towers and slowly place the large marshmallow on top of each team's structure to see if it will survive.

Discussion Questions

1. What was challenging about this problem?
2. What was your team's approach to solving this problem?
3. Did you brainstorm? How much time did you allocate to brainstorming?
4. Did your plan change along the way?
5. How did the team stay motivated throughout the process? Did the competition motivate you? Did the fact that it was a difficult challenge motivate you? Did the tight deadline motivate you?
6. What are some ways we can apply these motivators to our brainstorming sessions?

Cubing

OBJECTIVES
- To consider your brainstorming topic from six different perspectives
- To generate fresh ideas and uncover new connections

Group Size

Individual, or any size group

Materials

Principles of Cubing written on a flip chart or PowerPoint slide.

Time

20 minutes

Procedure

Cubing is a brainstorming strategy outlined in Gregory and Elizabeth Cowan's book *Writing* (New York: Wiley, 1980). Cubing enables you to consider your topic from six different directions; just as a cube is six-sided, your cubing brainstorm will result in six "sides" or approaches to the topic. Have individuals take a sheet of paper, consider the topic, and respond to these six principles of cubing, which you can write on a flip chart or transfer to a PowerPoint slide:

1. Describe it: What does it look like? What are its characteristics? Definitions? Parameters? What are the first things you notice about it?
2. Compare it: What is it similar to? Different from?
3. Associate it: What does it remind you of? How does it connect to you, the team, our workplace, our customers, the community? How does it connect with issues you have dealt with before? Does it remind you of anything you have worked on in the past?
4. Analyze it: Look deeper. What is it made of? How does is work? Can you identify the smaller parts that make up the whole? Is it possible to break it down into its components?

5. Apply it: What is it used for? How is it used? Who uses it?
6. Argue for and against it: Is it a good thing? A bad thing? Why?

Ask participants to reflect on what they have written. Now open it up to the group. Start your discussion by asking the following questions:

Discussion Questions

1. Do any of the responses suggest anything new about the topic?

2. What interactions do you notice among the sides of the cube? That is, do you see patterns repeating, or a theme emerging that we could use to approach the topic differently?

3. Did one side seem particularly helpful in getting your brain moving?

4. Could that one side help us draft a statement that will clarify our topic?

5. Use this technique in a way that serves your brainstorming topic best. At the very least, it will give your group members a broader awareness of your topic, and perhaps a keener understanding of what needs to happen next.

Squares and Triangles

OBJECTIVES
- To practice looking beyond the obvious
- To understand how different perspectives can be helpful in brainstorming

Group Size

Any

Materials

One Squares handout or one Triangles handout for each participant, pens

Time

10 to 15 minutes

Procedure

Choose either the Squares handout or the Triangles handout to distribute to everyone in your group. Use whichever you prefer; the rules and procedure for both handouts are the same. The instructions that follow are based on the Squares handout.

This game is played in four rounds:

Round 1—working individually, count the squares and write your answer on the handout.

Round 2—working with a partner, come to a consensus as to the number of squares and write your answer on the handout.

Round 3—working in teams of four or five, come to a consensus and write the answer on the handout.

Round 4—collaborate with another team (or teams) to ensure your team has found all the squares possible.

After the final round, have the group discuss what happened as they worked through each round. Draw their attention to the way in which the number of squares increased as more and more people came together to solve the problem. Brainstorming is about putting together single elements to obtain results greater than the sum of the single elements.

After discussing with the team, feel free to share this solution with them:

There are 40 squares:

- 1 large square
- 16 small squares
- 2 inner squares
- 8 smallest squares
- 9 2x2 squares
- 4 3x3 squares

Variation

For a different challenge, use the Triangle handout. There are 45 triangles:

- 1 large triangle
- 25 small triangles
- 10 triangles consisting of 4 small triangles
- 6 triangles consisting of 9 small triangles
- 3 triangles consisting of 16 small triangles

Discussion Questions

1. What were the results for each round?
2. How did your perception change as you collaborated with more and more people?
3. In what ways does collaboration benefit the team?
4. What is challenging about collaborating with others?
5. How can we promote collaboration within our team?
6. What characteristics encourage collaboration?

Squares

Count the squares you see in this drawing and write your answer for each round:

Round 1 _____

Round 2 _____

Round 3 _____

Round 4 _____

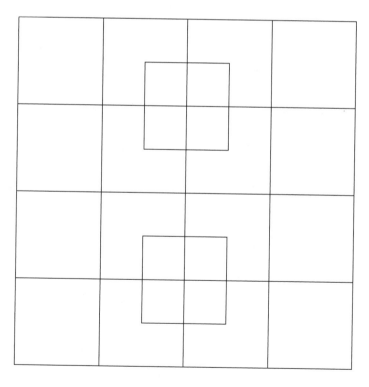

Triangles

Count the triangles you see in this drawing and write your answer for each round:

Round 1 _____

Round 2 _____

Round 3 _____

Round 4 _____

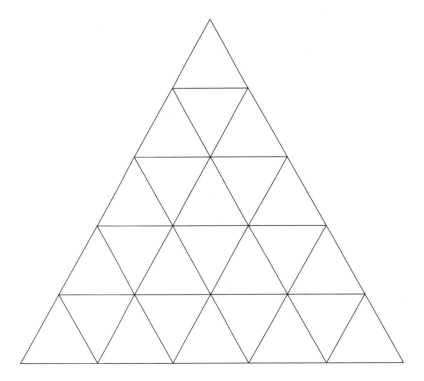

Everyone's Talking About It

OBJECTIVES

- To get everyone involved in the creation of a memorable group quote
- To discuss quotes from well-known innovators, creators, and leaders about creativity

Group Size

Any; split large groups into smaller teams of 4 to 6 participants

Materials

A copy of the Everyone's Talking About It handout for each group member

Time

20 minutes

Procedure

Split your group into smaller teams of four to six people. Give all group members a copy of the Everyone's Talking About It handout. Instruct them to take a few minutes individually to read through the list and reflect on the quotations from famous leaders and innovators. Have each team member identify one quotation from the list that is meaningful to him or her on a personal level. After a few minutes, have each member share with the team the quotation he or she chose, and explain why he or she chose it.

Next, have each team review the list of quotations together. Give them a few minutes to discuss and decide on just one quote that seems most meaningful or relevant to the entire group.

Finally, challenge teams to brainstorm and come up with a brand-new quote of their own. Their quotation should be about brainstorming, imagination, or creative thinking. Team members can borrow ideas from the Everyone's Talking About It handout, but their actual quotation must be in their own words.

Have all the teams rejoin into one large group, and give each team the opportunity to share their newly created quotation with the rest of the group.

Tips

Most teams will put real effort into creating a quotation that's meaningful for the group. Honor their work by posting the team quotations in a prominent place around the office, or by emailing a copy to everyone in the group.

Everyone's Talking About It

1. "You can't wait for inspiration, you have to go after it with a club."
   —Jack London

2. "Imagination is the living power and prime agent of all human perception."
   —Samuel Taylor Coleridge

3. "Creative thinking is not a talent, it is a skill that can be learnt. It empowers people by adding strength to their natural abilities which improves teamwork, productivity and where appropriate profits."
   —Edward de Bono

4. "There is no doubt that creativity is the most important human resource of all. Without creativity, there would be no progress, and we would be forever repeating the same patterns."
   —Edward de Bono

5. "Creativity is just connecting things."
   —Steve Jobs

6. "All great deeds and all great thoughts have a ridiculous beginning."
   —Albert Camus

7. "When you ask creative people how they did something, they feel a little guilty because they didn't really do it, they just saw something. It seemed obvious to them after a while. That's because they were able to connect experiences they've had and synthesize new things. And the reason they were able to do that was that they've had more experiences or they have thought more about their experiences than other people."
   —Steve Jobs

8. "It is not enough to just do your best or work hard. You must know what to work on."
   —W. Edwards Deming

9. "Genius is one percent inspiration, and ninety-nine percent perspiration."
   —Thomas Edison

10. "If at first the idea is not absurd, then there is no hope for it."
    —Albert Einstein

11. "Imagination is more important than knowledge. For while knowledge defines all we currently know and understand, imagination points to all we might yet discover and create."
    —Albert Einstein

12. "I can't understand why people are frightened of new ideas. I'm frightened of the old ones."
    —John Cage

13. "The creation of a thousand forests is in one acorn."
    —Ralph Waldo Emerson

14. "Whether you believe you can, or whether you believe you can't, you're absolutely right."
    —Henry Ford

15. "The broader one's understanding of the human experience, the better design we will have."
    —Steve Jobs

16. "A rock pile ceases to be a rock pile the moment a single man contemplates it, bearing within him the image of a cathedral."
    —Antoine de Saint-Exupéry

17. "Daring ideas are like chessmen moved forward. They may be beaten, but they may start a winning game."
    —Johann Wolfgang von Goethe

18. "I began by tinkering around with some old tunes I knew. Then, just to try something different, I set to putting some music to the rhythm that I used in jerking ice-cream sodas at the Poodle Dog. I fooled around with the tune more and more until at last, lo and behold, I had completed my first piece of finished music."
    —Duke Ellington

19. "I used to think anyone doing anything weird was weird. Now I know that it is the people that call others weird that are weird."
    —Paul McCartney

20. "If I have seen further it is by standing on the shoulders of giants."
    —Isaac Newton

21. "Ideas are like rabbits. You get a couple and learn how to handle them, and pretty soon you have a dozen."
    —John Steinbeck

22. "Simple can be harder than complex: You have to work hard to get your thinking clean to make it simple. But it's worth it in the end because once you get there, you can move mountains."
    —Steve Jobs

23. "The best way to get a good idea is to get a lot of ideas."
    —Linus Pauling

24. "Few people think more than two or three times a year. I've made an international reputation for myself by thinking once or twice a week."
    —George Bernard Shaw

25. "Our life is frittered away by detail. . . . Simplify, simplify."
    —Henry Thoreau

26. "The man with a new idea is a crank—until the idea succeeds."
    —Mark Twain

27. "It's fine to celebrate success but it is more important to heed the lessons of failure."
    —Bill Gates

28. "God is really another artist. He invented the giraffe, the elephant, and the cat. He has no real style. He just goes on trying other things."
    —Pablo Picasso

29. "We keep moving forward, opening new doors, and doing new things, because we're curious and curiosity keeps leading us down new paths."
    —Walt Disney

30. "The creative is the place where no one else has ever been. You have to leave the city of your comfort and go into the wilderness of your intuition. What you'll discover will be wonderful. What you'll discover is yourself."
    —Alan Alda

Inside the Box

OBJECTIVES

- To generate more ideas in a brainstorming session
- To understand the different modes and styles of brainstorming

Group Size

Individual, or any size group

Materials

Inside the Box handout, assorted magazines, pencils or pens for each participant

Time

20 minutes

Procedure

Email the Inside the Box handout to everyone in the group. Tell them to set aside ten minutes prior to the brainstorming session to fill in as many of the boxes as they can. Encourage them to draw, doodle, write, or use any creative method they wish in order to complete the handout.

Have everyone bring their completed handouts to the brainstorming session. During the session, have them refer to their handouts as they contribute to the discussion. A fun twist is to have them switch handouts halfway through the activity and try to interpret the new handout from their own personal perspective. This can sometimes lead to the generation of new and original ideas!

Variations

You can use this handout with the "Pass It & Plus It" technique. Present the problem, then have everyone fill in one of the boxes. Group members pass the handout to their right, the next person completes a box, and so on until they get their original handout back again or until all the boxes are complete. Whatever handout they end up with is the one they can use to help guide their contributions in the brainstorming session. Request they fill in a different spot for each handout.

Inside the Box

Doodle it

?

Dictionary

OBJECTIVES
- To generate different ideas
- To increase creative thinking

Group Size

Individual, or groups of 4 to 7

Materials

Dictionary (not an online version)

Time

10 minutes

Procedure

For this activity, you will be using the old-school version of a dictionary. You remember those, don't you?

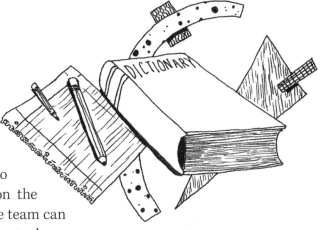

Any brainstorming session should include a dictionary. We like to have one sitting right on the middle of the table so the team can easily use it when they are stuck, or even just to get the ideas flowing. With today's technology, it's easy to look up words, but this activity isn't about looking up word definitions. In this activity, you will be using random words as spark plugs to ignite creative thinking.

Begin by stating the brainstorming topic. Once the team has clearly defined the topic, have one person open the dictionary to a random page and point to a word and say it out loud. The team now has to solve their problem with the word chosen. Use the principle of force fitting. If the team can't think of anything right away when presented with the particular word chosen, keep at it until you get responses. Using this technique forces the team to go beyond the easy, obvious ideas.

Variations

You can also use magazines. Have a team member open a magazine to a random page and point to a picture (for example, a bike). This is a great way to add a visual component to the process. Build a collection of different types of magazines such as home improvement, architecture, fashion, and sports magazines.

Tips

Stick with words that generate pictures in the team members' minds. Those words would typically be nouns.

9

The Dynamics of Involvement

We keep moving forward, opening new doors, and doing new things, because we're curious and curiosity keeps leading us down new paths.

—Walt Disney

Poetry in Motion (Not for the Faint of Heart)

OBJECTIVE
- To build your creative muscle
- To build resources for idea generation

Group Size

Individual

Materials

Paper and pen

Time

One hour or more, but you're worth it!

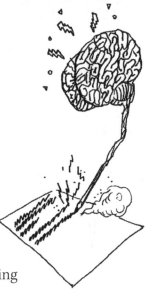

Process

Individuals can use this technique to tap into their personal creativity. It can be used to stimulate individual thinking or can even be used by team members before the group meets to generate some ideas before they come to the brainstorming session.

The first step is to choose something to write about. We recommend considering the things you love to do or an object or place that has a special meaning for you. Ideally, you want to pick something that inspires you, something you could talk about for hours. For example, it could be the Grand Canyon, rock climbing, motorcycles, or poodles.

Now that you have your favorite thing in mind, sit down with a blank paper and a pen. Now write. Write about your subject, write about your day, write whatever pops into your mind. When you can't think of anything else to write, then write that, too. This technique is called *freewriting*. Freewriting is writing without stopping to make corrections, without stopping to make sense, without stopping for any reason at all. Just keep going. If you can't think of anything else to write, then you simply write, "I can't think of anything else to write." Let the momentum carry you through to (perhaps) a breakthrough. Write for ten minutes without stopping. This takes discipline, but we have faith in you—you can do it!

The next step is to broaden your perspective on your subject. Go to the local library and do some research, go online to look it up, pull out an old dictionary and look it up. Do you have any old encyclopedias lying around? Great! What can you find there? What is the history behind it? What is the science involved? When was it discovered? By whom? Continue to ask questions such as these until you are completely immersed in your subject.

At this point, you have a large amount of information. Gather your written notes along with any other materials you collected and see if you can put it all together . . . in a poem. That's right, a poem. Blend or mix up the information and your thoughts and feelings into a poem. It can be as long or as short as you would like it to be. The point is to stretch your comfort zone, practice creativity, and do something completely out of character. By going through this process, you are feeding the passion within you, but you are also getting outside yourself by searching for material beyond your personal experience. Then you are connecting all that great stuff to create your "masterpiece."

That's Exactly What It Is!

OBJECTIVES
- To support others' ideas
- To be creative in a silly way

Group Size

Up to 20

Materials

One bandanna

Time

10 minutes

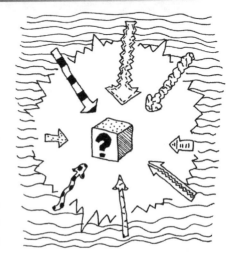

Procedure

Have the team stand in a circle. Before you begin the game, tell the team that the feedback or response to whatever another person says during the game is, "That's exactly what it is!" Model saying the words with gusto, and request that the team members say this phrase with enthusiasm in their voice and body language. Have the team say the phrase, giving lots of praise for their level of excitement.

Next, take the bandanna and wave it high above your head, saying, "This is a kite!" To which the team responds, "That's exactly what it is!" Pass it to the person on your right, and whatever they choose to have the bandanna signify, reply with enthusiasm, "That's exactly what it is!" Continue all the way around the circle, giving everyone a chance to create something from the bandanna.

Tips

Your level of excitement will set the stage, so get enthusiastic and be ridiculous with your example. Position yourself so the person who gets the bandanna after you is a naturally outgoing person who will jump right in, match your enthusiasm, and play along.

Creative Man!

OBJECTIVE
- To understand the ways in which we are all creative

Group Size

Any

Materials

One Creative Man! handout

Time

15 minutes

Procedure

You have all heard of Superman, Spider-Man, Batman, and even Wonder Woman, but have you heard of Creative Man? Creative Man has super-creative powers. He doesn't need a phone booth to transform, he doesn't need any box at all; in fact, he is always "outside the box" when it comes to thinking. Creative Man is far superior to other super heroes because he is able and willing to share his creative superpowers with all of us!

For this prime-the-pump activity, have group members complete the Creative Man! questionnaire. When everyone is finished, have them work in pairs to discuss how they answered the questions and discuss any similarities. Follow with a group discussion using the handout to guide you. One question you can add to your group discussion is, "How can we support each other in being more creative together?"

The idea is that we are all creative; in fact, the business world with all its dynamic people and processes is the ultimate creative challenge! Use the following handout to help your team recognize the ways in which they are creative.

Creative Man!

When was the last time you came up with a creative idea?

☐ This morning
☐ Yesterday
☐ Last week
☐ Last month
☐ Last year

What was it? _____

What motivates you to be creative? _____

Ways I'm creative at home _____

Ways I'm creative at work _____

What I enjoy most about being creative _____

What I enjoy least about being creative _____

How I feel when I am being creative _____

Three things I fear about being creative:

_____

_____

_____

_____

Your Biggest Fan

OBJECTIVES
- A fresh perspective on competition
- Create an atmosphere of complete acceptance

Group Size

At least 20

Materials

None

Time

10 minutes

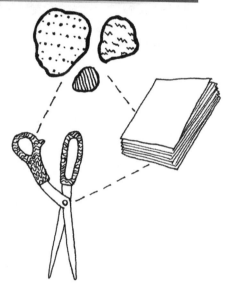

Procedure

Ask the team if anyone knows how to play Roshambo. Roshambo is the "formal" name for Rock, Paper, Scissors. Usually, someone in the group knows this and can explain it to the rest of the participants. Have the team members find partners and ask that they go over the rules of Roshambo. For consistency in this competition, request that the teams follow this procedure: 1, 2, 3, show! And show either rock, paper, or scissors.

The partners play the best two out of three. As soon as one of the partners wins the competition, the other person immediately turns into the winner's biggest fan. They could shout their name, pat them on the back, say, "You are the best Roshambo player in the world!" yell "Yay!" or exhibit any other demonstration of pure fan behavior. The bigger, louder, and more exaggerated the praise, the better.

The next step is for the winner to compete against another winner from the crowd. The new contender will also have his or her own cheering section from the previous round. The two new players square off, and when one person wins, the remaining three players square off, and when one person wins, the remaining three become the cheering section for this winner. Play subsequent rounds in the same way. As winners eliminate contenders, their cheering section grows. Play this until there is one single winner. End the game with the entire room cheering in unison for the ultimate champion.

Tips
Make sure everyone is using names to recognize the winners.

I've Got Your Back

OBJECTIVES
- To get everyone involved in the process
- To check our egos at the door!

Group Size

Any

Materials

None

Time

15 to 30 minutes before the meeting; 20 to 30 minutes during the meeting

Procedure

This activity serves three purposes. It gives quieter group members an opportunity to have their ideas represented, it allows all ideas to be shared without being attached to any one person, and it creates an atmosphere of trust and respect.

Assign each team member a partner. Give the team members the brainstorming topic ahead of time and let them know who their partner is. Have them schedule a 15- to 30-minute meeting with their partner to be held prior to the group's brainstorming session.

Ask team members to spend some time thinking about the topic, to collect their thoughts regarding the topic, and come prepared with some ideas when meeting with their partner. Tell them to consider how they would like those thoughts represented by their partner.

Give group members time to think/brainstorm/generate ideas individually.

Split them into groups of two. It's best if nobody knows who is partnered with whom. Each pair meets to share their ideas with their partner. Partners are encouraged to ask questions, take notes, ask for examples, request feedback, and do whatever it takes to fully understand the other's position or idea. This part of the exercise is important, so allow as much time as necessary for everyone to become familiar with his or her partner's position.

Have everyone gather as a group for the brainstorming session. One at a time, have people share, describe, and advocate their partner's position to the rest of the group. They should not tell the rest of the group who their partner is. They should take on the role of being their partner's spokesperson, being sure to accurately represent the thoughts and ideas of their partner.

After all ideas have been fully presented, allow group members to add and comment.

Proceed as you would with your brainstorming session.

My Professional Opinion

OBJECTIVES
- To generate many diverse ideas
- To see things from a different perspective

Group Size

Any, split into teams of 4 to 12 participants

Materials

None

Time

30 minutes

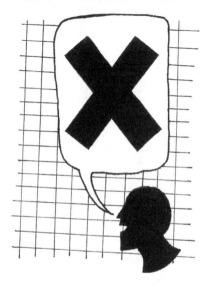

Procedure

An effective way to broaden your understanding of a topic is to look at the situation from a different point of view. For this brainstorming technique, assign each small work team a different occupation. See the list on the next page for some suggestions.

While brainstorming, have each team of 4 to 12 consider how someone of their assigned occupation would approach the problem. Have group members ask themselves these types of questions:

- What knowledge would they bring to the problem? (Academic or real-world street smarts?)
- How would they think? (Concretely? Abstractly?)
- What experiences would they draw from? (Do they have experience with this issue or would they bring a fresh perspective?)
- What would they do? (Would they take time to plan or jump right into action?)
- How would they define the problem? (Process, people, product, or pressure?)

- What solutions would they consider? (Quick, easy answers or more complicated solutions)
- How would they make decisions? (Involve everyone or decide on their own?)
- Where would they be solving the problem? (Indoors, outdoors, at a computer?)
- What tools would they use? (Words, images, machines, technology)

Challenge the group to see how many different ways they think someone from the selected profession would approach the problem. See how many ideas and solutions they can generate.

Occupations:

1. History professor
2. Firefighter
3. Mathematician
4. Team-building facilitator
5. Professional athlete (specify)
6. Police officer
7. Pilates instructor
8. Kindergarten teacher
9. Mechanical engineer
10. DMV employee
11. Farmer
12. Letter carrier
13. Politician
14. Garbage collector
15. Coffee barista
16. Customer service representative
17. Car salesperson
18. Banker
19. Medical doctor
20. Social media specialist
21. Computer software engineer
22. Lawyer
23. Credit and collections manager

Variations

You can use this method in a few different ways:

1. Individually you can choose a profession and imagine how that person would approach the problem and the different ideas they would generate.
2. With a team, you could have the entire group assume the same profession.

10

Things Look Different from Here

A rock pile ceases to be a rock pile the moment a single man contemplates it, bearing within him the image of a cathedral.

— Antoine de Saint-Exupéry

Just One Word

OBJECTIVES
- To look at things differently
- To build creative problem-solving muscles

Group Size

Any

Materials

Puzzle #1 and Puzzle #2 handouts (cut apart to separate), pens or pencils

Time

15 minutes

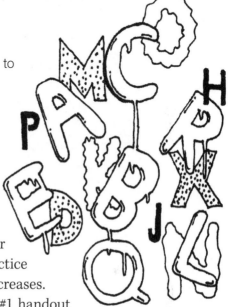

Procedure

It is often said that creativity is like a muscle. Practice creativity a lot and you become better and stronger at coming up with ideas. Don't practice and your ability to generate ideas decreases.

Give group members the Puzzle #1 handout and let everyone work on it individually for three to five minutes. After three to five minutes, have them set aside Puzzle #1. At this point, distribute the Puzzle #2 handout. For Puzzle #2, team members can work together and share ideas freely. After they have discovered the solution to Puzzle #2, have them return to Puzzle #1, and again working individually, see how long it takes them to figure out the solution that may have eluded them the first time.

Variations

You can easily present both puzzles using a PowerPoint slide or flip chart. Have group members work alone for a few minutes on Puzzle #1, then replace it with Puzzle #2 and follow the same instructions as above.

Spoiler Alert! Answers to the Puzzles

Puzzle #1: The letters spell "JUST ONE WORD"

Puzzle #2: Cross out "S I X L E T T E R S" and you are left with "ONE WORD."

Discussion Questions

1. Did the second puzzle help to solve the first puzzle? Why?
2. Did you experience a shift in your thinking during the time we spent on the puzzles?
3. In what ways do challenges such as these build our brainstorming muscles?

Puzzle #1

Use the letters below to spell out just one word.

D E J N O O R S T U W

Puzzle #2

Cross out six letters to reveal one word.

S O I N X L E T E W T O E R R D S

5-Postcard Draw

OBJECTIVE
- To use the force-fitting principle as a means to generate fresh ideas

Group Size

Individual, or teams of 3 to 5

Materials

Assorted postcards (enough so you have at least one for each person)

Time

10 minutes

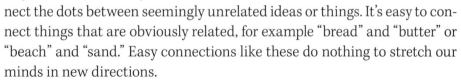

Procedure

The force-fitting principle is a way to build our ability to connect the dots between seemingly unrelated ideas or things. It's easy to connect things that are obviously related, for example "bread" and "butter" or "beach" and "sand." Easy connections like these do nothing to stretch our minds in new directions.

When we travel, we often pick up postcards to signify the new places we have experienced. Just like travel takes you to new places, this activity takes you to new brainstorming places. Split your group into smaller teams of three to five people. Give each team three to five postcards. Don't let them choose (this is the "forcing" part). Instead, keep the postcards facedown and hand them out randomly.

Once they have their cards, each team must build a scenario that combines all the cards into a cohesive story that connects to its brainstorming issue.

Variations

You can use magazine pictures or photos from the web or even have everyone bring a postcard with them (mix them up before you pass them out so they don't necessarily get their own postcard).

Tips

When you are out and about, go into a bookstore or card shop and buy some interesting postcards. We like the postcards that have images that are metaphorical, such as pictures of hands, bridges, ladders, water, snakes, eyes, or ears, in addition to the more traditional postcards. You will be pleasantly surprised at the stories your groups come up with.

First Impressions

OBJECTIVE
- To understand how barriers, either real or perceived, impact creativity

Group Size

Any

Materials

One copy of the Hermann Grid and the Kanizsa Triangle handouts for each participant

Time

10 minutes

Procedure

This activity provides an excellent example of how we sometimes see things that do not exist. We may create boundaries, obstacles, and parameters that serve to stifle our creativity. Give each team member a copy of the Hermann Grid handout and a copy of the Kanizsa Triangle handout. In teams of four to seven participants, have them share their first impressions of the image on the pages. Ask if they see any gray dots in the white spaces. Ask if they see the center triangle where none is drawn, and if so, is it the same color as the surrounding area?

Tips

For large groups, pass out a set of discussion questions to each small team of four to seven, to discuss prior to the group debriefing discussion.

Discussion Questions

1. What do you "see" in the two pictures?

2. In the Hermann Grid are the gray dots really there?

3. What do the gray dots and the phantom triangle signify for your team? Do we see potential or do we see distractions? How might this influence our creativity?

The Hermann Grid

(named after Ludimar Hermann)

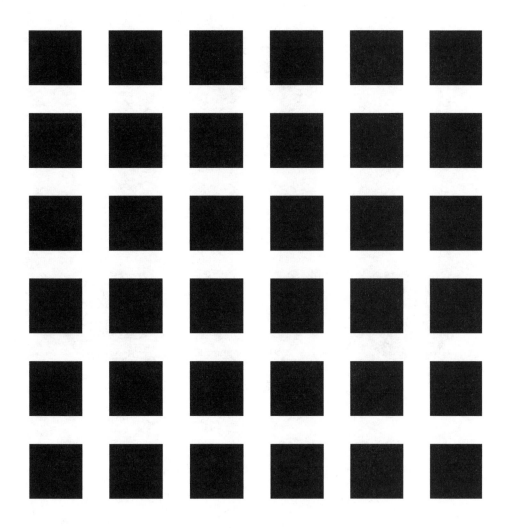

The Kanizsa Triangle

(first described by Gaetano Kanizsa in 1955)

Colors

OBJECTIVES
- To consider common things in an uncommon way
- To broaden team members' perspectives

Group Size

Any

Materials

One copy of the Colors handout

Time

10 minutes

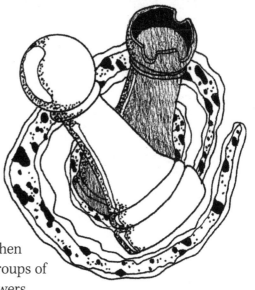

Procedure

Pass out the handout or transfer the questions to a flip chart or slide. Give participants five minutes to answer the questions. When the time is up, have them form groups of four to seven to discuss their answers.

Discussion Questions

1. Did everyone agree on the answers?
2. Who was "right"?
3. Were you critical of other people's answers? Why or why not?
4. How can we carry the same acceptance into brainstorming sessions?
5. What agreements can we make before we begin to brainstorm?
6. In what ways does color impact your creativity?
7. How can you change your environment so you feel more creative?

Colors

1. What color is happiness? _____

2. What color is sadness? _____

3. What color is tenderness? _____

4. What color is loneliness? _____

5. What color is excitement? _____

6. What color is creativity? _____

7. What color is intelligence? _____

8. What color is love? _____

9. What is your favorite color? _____

10. What is your least favorite color? _____

Turn It on Its Head

OBJECTIVES
- To gain a different perspective
- To understand the different types of creativity

Group Size

Any

Materials

Drawing handout, pens and paper

Time

10 minutes

Procedure

Tell the team you will be testing to see if there are any truly creative people in the group. Show them the handout and give them five minutes to re-create the drawing. Have the team members show their drawings to each other. Now ask them to turn their paper over. Once again show them the drawing, but this time, hold it upside down. Ask them to once again re-create the picture. Have the team compare the results with the first drawing.

Variations

Rather than use the template, I like to get the team involved from the start by asking a person from the group with artistic talents in illustration to draw the original.

Discussion Questions

1. Were your results different? Why?
2. Which was easier? Why do you think that was?
3. What does this tell us about creativity?
4. In what ways can we apply this method to enhance creativity in the workplace?

Today's Guest Speaker

OBJECTIVES
- To approach problems from a different perspective
- To "let the idea" win

Group Size
Any
Materials
None
Time
20 to 30 minutes

Procedure

This activity is a variation of the creative problem-solving strategy that involves asking a question like, "How would Bill Gates solve this?" or "How would a fashion model do it?" But in this case, you will be asking a real person.

To gain new ideas or a fresh approach, invite someone from a different discipline to your brainstorming session. Someone from a different department would be good; someone from another company would be better; best would be a person from a different and unrelated field.

This activity involves some prework on your or the team's part, to give the guest plenty of time to make arrangements so he or she can be present in person. Tap into the connections of the team members. Whom do they know? What do their neighbors do?

You can invite the person to your workplace or select a "meet in the middle" location such as a coffeehouse.

When you invite your guest, you want that person to become somewhat familiar with the topic, but make sure not to give too much information because you want your guest's unique perspective.

Consider including this information in your invitation:

- Your challenge: state it in three sentences.
- The request: ask for 30 minutes of his or her time.
- Expectations: expert does not need to be able to answer all questions.
- Encourage guest to build on ideas in the brainstorming session.

As facilitator, encourage your team to be polite. This will contribute to a nonjudgmental acceptance of ideas. We encourage the team to participate in the discussion. Involve everyone so that your guest does not feel put on the spot. As facilitator, be ready to create a smooth process for all involved. The outside perspective may shine a spotlight on new ideas, raise new questions, get your team out of a rut, or reveal a unique solution to your problem.

Field Trip

OBJECTIVES
- To explore new ways of looking at a problem or challenge
- To be inspired by the good ideas of other organizations

Group Size

Any

Materials

None

Time

60 minutes to several hours

Procedure

To gain a fresh perspective on your brainstorming topic, hit the road and take your group on an idea-gathering field trip. You may be surprised by the insights you can gain by getting out and observing the ways organizations from different industries tackle challenges like yours.

To get the most from this off-site activity, spend some time preparing. You should be clear about your purpose. Make sure every group member has a solid understanding of your brainstorming topic. Remind everyone that this will be a field trip with a very specific purpose.

Do some research to identify places or organizations that have something in common with the focus of your brainstorming topic. Suppose the subject of your brainstorming is "How can we provide customers at our hardware store with the best customer service ever?" You will want to look for places and organizations from various industries that deal with customers every day. For example, each of the places listed below has a unique way of serving their customers. What can your group learn from a visit to:

- Your local coffeehouse
- Nordstrom's (or other department store)

- A used-car dealer
- Yoga studio
- A local children's hospital
- Apple store (or other computer store)
- Department of Motor Vehicles
- Fast-food restaurant
- High-end jewelry store

It is courteous to give a call before your visit to let them know you are coming. Try to arrange a behind-the-scenes tour. You will find that most people will be flattered that you singled out their organization for a visit and will be happy to show you around.

During your visit, spend time talking to lots of people, including front-line workers and mid- and top-level managers, as well as customers. Come prepared with questions that are relevant to your brainstorming subject: "How do you deal with our types of issues?" "How does your team come up with good ideas?" "Why do you do this the way you do?" Jot down notes, take pictures (with management's permission, of course), and record whatever observations will be helpful with your topic.

After your visit, schedule a meeting with your brainstorming group to debrief the experience and talk about what everyone learned. Do this within a day or two of your visit while the details are still fresh in everyone's minds. Use the insights you gained and the good ideas you observed to help generate a list of creative ideas that will lead to a great solution for your group's challenge.

Playable Clayables

OBJECTIVES
- To demonstrate how tangible, tactile items can be helpful for brainstorming
- To use Play-Doh to visualize, conceptualize, or clarify your group's specific challenge

Group Size

Individual, or teams of up to 5

Materials

Play-Doh (or a similar sculpting clay product), plus a disposable work surface for covering desktops and keeping things from getting messy (such as paper, cardboard, or a tarp)

Time

45 to 60 minutes

Procedure

This activity gives group members a chance to roll up their sleeves to creatively explore their brainstorming problem or challenge. Borrowing from the playbook of product designers, architects, furniture makers, and engineers, they will build a mock-up model representing your brainstorming subject. Don't let the fact that you will be doing it with Play-Doh fool you—although it is lots of fun, this activity is far from silly! The use of tangible building materials forces groups to think about their brainstorming topic in concrete, tangible ways that can lead to valuable insights and true breakthroughs in thinking.

Split the group into small teams of up to five people each. Give each team four or more cans of Play-Doh in assorted colors. Clearly state the subject of your brainstorming session. Tell the teams that although most brainstorming sessions involve verbalizing ideas using words, today they will visualize their ideas and build models of them using something, in this case, children's sculpting clay.

Give teams about 30 minutes to explore their ideas visually using the Play-Doh. Tell them there are no rules to restrict their imagination. They can super-size a feature of their model to emphasize its importance, use different colors to represent different aspects of the object, or do whatever they wish to create a mock-up that's meaningful for the team. Their model can be a very concrete representation of the subject, or it can be abstract.

For example, suppose your brainstorming goal is to make your company's line of golf carts the best designed, most innovative in the world. Teams could use their Play-Doh to visualize a sleeker, more streamlined golf cart that will be popular with style-conscious golfers. They could add crazy or never-before-seen features, perhaps creating a Play-Doh model of an all-terrain, amphibious golf cart that can zip across lakes or water traps as easily as it moves across solid ground (useful for retrieving stray golf balls or beating another team to the next hole!).

Encourage everyone on the team to contribute ideas. It is not necessary for each team member to actually work with the Play-Doh, but it is essential for everyone to participate in the brainstorming process. Remind participants to contribute as many ideas as they can, and to build on each other's thoughts. Wild and original ideas are welcome. Discourage negative comments or criticism.

After everyone has finished building their Play-Doh models, have each team present their models to the rest of the group. Instruct them to point out the key features of their model, and have them explain some of the important decisions that were made during the process. Let each team decide the best way to present and describe their model to the group. After each team presents their Play-Doh model, give them some time to answer questions from the rest of the group.

Variations

Try replacing Play-Doh with other kinds of building toys like Legos, Lincoln Logs, or Tinkertoys. You can also gain similar results using items from an arts and crafts store.

The Other Side

OBJECTIVE
• To practice listening and making connections

Group Size

Up to 40

Materials

One copy of the book *The Other Side* by Istvan Banyai. To prepare the book for this game, remove the binding and cover so that only the individual pages with illustrations remain.

Time

20 minutes

Procedure

Here is an excellent perspective activity that also stimulates creative thinking and looking beyond the obvious. It's also a great game to introduce the idea of making connections to generate ideas while brainstorming.

In Istvan Banyai's *The Other Side* (Chronicle Books), each page of the book contains a scene. The flip side of the page shows that same scene, but from a different perspective. For example, on one side of the page, you see a little boy looking out the window and the opposite side shows the inside of a little boy's bedroom. The same scene is illustrated from two different perspectives.

To begin, have everyone find a partner and sit or stand face-to-face. Have the partners hold the page between them so they can only look at their side of the page. Their task is to talk about what they see on their side of the page, listen to their partner's perspective, and discuss ways in which the scenes are related. Ultimately, the goal is to figure out between them what story makes the two pictures connect and make sense.

Discussion Questions

1. What are some things that lead to different perspectives?

2. How do we benefit from considering another viewpoint?

3. What is the best way to incorporate this quality into our brainstorming sessions?

4. What norms could we create to support those qualities?

11

What Seems to Be the Problem?

You can't wait for inspiration, you have to go after it with a club.

—*Jack London*

Simply Put

OBJECTIVES
- To draft a concise problem statement
- To create ownership of the goal

Group Size

Up to 10

Materials

Flip-chart paper; black markers for each person; one red, blue, and green marker; tape

Time

20 minutes

Procedure

> Give me a problem well defined
> and therein lies the solution.
> —*Robert Louis Stevenson*

This is a great way to simplify complex issues. Much like having a clear goal, the more clearly defined the problem, the easier it is for team members to brainstorm a solution. Challenge your group to come up with a simple and clear problem definition using this activity.

To start, give each person a sheet of flip-chart paper and a marker (check to make sure the markers don't bleed through to the wall). Have them post their papers throughout the room. Individually, each person writes his or her 15-word interpretation of the goal in large letters on his or her page. The letters need to be big enough for the rest of the team to see. When all the participants are finished, have them line up their pages in a row on one wall. Allow a few minutes for the group to read all the statements. Then ask them as a group to use a red marker to underline common words, themes, or phrases that best define the goal. Ask them to use a green marker to circle "fuzzy" or unclear language and then clarify. Ask them to use a blue marker to put a check by any wording that creates concern within the team.

Discuss areas of disagreement using open-ended questions, such as, "What are some reasons you see the problem this way?" or "What are some reasons we should include this in our statement?"

Work as a team to craft a goal statement that uses the underlined, circled, and checked words in a way that defines the problem clearly and simply.

This process is an effective way to engage all team members and ultimately come up with a goal statement all team members feel a sense of ownership for. By spending the time clearly defining the problem, you have also planted seeds for the brainstorming solutions. All the while the team members are rewording the problem, their minds are considering solutions.

Cut, Cut, Cut!

OBJECTIVES
- To practice simplicity
- To clarify the goal or issue

Group Size
Any
Materials
Stopwatch
Time
10 minutes

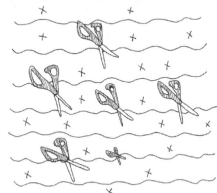

Procedure

At the start of your brainstorming session, take a full minute to present the goal/issue/problem. The person leading the session should practice so that he or she is able to fill the entire minute explaining the problem in detail. Now ask for a brave volunteer to reexplain the problem in 30 seconds. Ask for another volunteer to narrow it down to 15 seconds. The last individual volunteer has 7.5 seconds to give his or her summary of the problem. Be sure to lead the team in plenty of well-deserved applause after each volunteer has presented his or her rendition of the original problem. Encourage your volunteers to take a bow as they receive their accolades. By now the team should have a pretty good idea of what is involved, so, as a final step, have teams of three or four participants come up with a 3.75-second version of the problem. Have the group choose the version that states the problem most accurately. Now you are ready to brainstorm!

Follow with the brainstorming session. After the session, you may want to ask some discussion questions regarding the simplification process you used to start the ideas flowing.

Discussion Question

1. In what ways did taking some time to clarify the issue help brainstorm?

Airing of the Grievances

OBJECTIVES
- To gain confidence and control
- To develop a problem-solving attitude

Group Size

Individually, or small teams of 4 to 6

Materials

One copy per partners of Airing of the Grievances handout, pens or pencils

Time

10 to 30 minutes

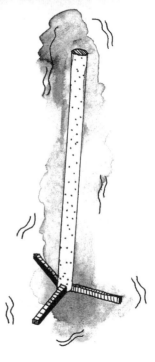

Procedure

Thanks to the popular sitcom *Seinfeld*, "Festivus" has become a well-known holiday un-celebration. You can even purchase Festivus poles to assist in the merriment. Part of Festivus is the *airing of the grievances*, where un-celebrators have the opportunity to clear the air regarding how the other people in attendance have bothered them throughout the past year. For this game, we are not targeting other people; we are targeting processes, product, and pressures as the object of our displeasure. More specifically, we are focusing on specific categories to ignite fresh perspectives and ideas.

This Festivus-like activity can be played individually or with a group. To make the most of the airing of the grievances, encourage your group to have some fun with it, to really get into the indignity of it all.

The grievance categories are:

- Process—What bugs us about our process?
- Product—What is the most undesirable feature of our product (consider what customers complain about)?
- Pressures—What takes too much time? What demands are overwhelming us?

Record the grievances. Spend some time discussing them and choose the three grievances that are the biggest obstacles to success. Once the team has identified their top three grievances, go back through and rewrite them as action questions that can provide insights into possible solutions.

- Process—What can we do to make it better, faster, more streamlined?
- Product—What can we add, subtract, or change to make it better?
- Pressures—How can we manage time more effectively? How can we work together to meet demands in a timely manner?

What happens when we do this? We gain control; we gain confidence. We are no longer victims of circumstance, but creators of our future. You can use the template provided, or just sit down with a blank piece of paper (preferred method). Using the blank piece of paper puts the pressure on a little, so perhaps save this method for the second time you go through this activity.

When to use this? Anytime you or the group catch yourselves in "poor us" mode, grab a paper and pen and get to work.

Airing of the Grievances

Please write down as many grievances as you can think of right now. When you are done, go back and rewrite your grievances as action questions, beginning with the word *how*.

Grievances	Action Questions
I can never find a decent parking spot when I get to work.	How can I ensure I get a close parking spot every day?

12

After the Storm

Simple can be harder than complex: You have to work hard to get your thinking clean to make it simple. But it's worth it in the end because once you get there, you can move mountains.

—*Steve Jobs*

That Will Never Work Around Here

OBJECTIVES

- To create an action plan
- To experience the "turn it on its head" method of creativity

Group Size

Any

Materials

That Will Never Work Around Here handout, pens

Time

20 minutes

Procedure

After your group comes up with a solution or goal based on the brainstorming session, a fun and effective way to increase the probability action is taken is to have the group come up with all the reasons the idea will never work. Obstacles often occur during the action stage. Using this game will allow the group to consider what those obstacles could be and create a game plan for working through them. The added benefit is the sense of control the group feels when they encounter a setback, rather then allowing themselves to get derailed during the process.

Use the handout on the next page. Follow the same procedure you do for brainstorming: generate lots of ideas for why your solution won't work. Record the ideas in the first column under the heading, "That will never work around here because." Make sure the ideas are clearly stated. After your team has exhausted all the possible reasons the solution won't work, move on to the second column, "Well, maybe it *could* work if we." Here, record the group's ideas for ways to manipulate or alter the solution to overcome the obstacle stated in the first column. Finally, in the third column, have the group change it into an action statement that will make it work. You will find examples in the handout.

"That will never work around here!"

That will never work around here because:	Well, maybe it *could* work here if we:	And to make it work we could:
We don't have the money in our budget.	Split the process into two phases.	Implement phase one this quarter, phase two next quarter.

And the Winner Is . . .

OBJECTIVES

- To provide structure to your brainstorming session
- To create an action plan after you have finished brainstorming

Group Size

Any, split into groups of 4 to 7

Materials

Paper, pens, whiteboard or flip chart, markers, timers

Time

45 minutes

Procedure

To guide your group(s) through an entire brainstorming session, follow these five steps:

1. Define the problem (use the In What Ways? activity on page 89)
2. Set a timer for 25 minutes. During that time, the goal is to generate at least 100 ideas. For most groups, the first 20 to 30 ideas are easy; it gets progressively more challenging after that. After about 20 minutes, ideas may even start to seem downright silly. Beware of cutting the activity short at this point, because this is when some of the most creative ideas are generated. In fact, the last five minutes of a brainstorming session are sometimes referred to as the "magic five minutes."
3. From the list of 100 ideas, choose your top five ideas.
4. Identify criteria by which the ideas will be measured. For example: cost effective, easy to implement, able to be completed by a certain date, doable with the resources we have access to.
5. Score each idea on a scale of 1 to 5 for each criterion.

AND THE WINNER IS . . .

The one that scored the most points! Congratulations! You have identified your group's best idea!

Affinity Sort

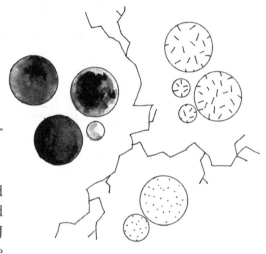

Group Size
Up to 10

Materials
Index cards, pens or pencils

Time
10 to 30 minutes

Procedure

The affinity diagram was devised by Kawakita Jiro in the 1960s and is sometimes referred to as the KJ Method. This process can create greater buy-in and accountability among group members.

Here's how your group can use it to organize their ideas after their brainstorming session.

1. Put each idea on a separate index card. Clarify ideas as you go, writing each idea as a word or a phrase. Have everybody on the team grab a pen or pencil and help out. Request they write the ideas legibly.
2. Randomly lay all the cards on a large table.
3. Sort the ideas. For this step, it's best to keep the discussion at a minimum. Tell the team, "Without speaking, sort the cards into groups based on your initial gut reaction. If you don't like the placement of a certain card, move it. We are going to continue until we reach consensus. We are looking for between five- and ten-card groupings."
4. If an idea relates to more than one category or group, and consensus can't be reached, make a second card and place it in both groups.

5. Take a look at the groupings. If one group is particularly large, ask the team to consider splitting it into two smaller groups.
6. Create header cards for the groupings. Headers should be concise; fewer than five words are best. Place the header cards at the top of each grouping.
7. Document the finished Affinity Sort diagram. Start with your problem statement, then your headers, and finally the ideas.
8. Develop an action plan.

Affinity Sort

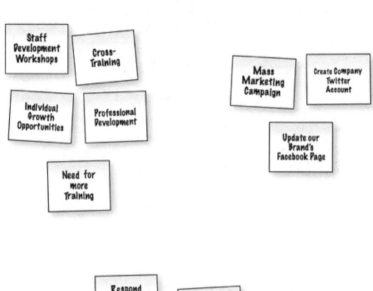

What Could Go Wrong?

OBJECTIVES
- To create buyin to the solution
- To establish an action plan

Group Size

Up to 12

Materials

What Could Go Wrong?
handout, pens

Time

20 minutes

Procedure

This process helps a team discover things that could possibly go wrong when implementing their solution they have agreed upon. It allows a team to look at problems from a fresh perspective and identify potential obstacles before they occur, so rather than being taken by surprise when problems arise, the team feels a sense of control during implementation. After the team has brainstormed a solution, follow these steps:

1. Write the solution at the top of the page.
2. Ask the group, "What can we do to ensure we do not achieve the desired result?"
3. Write down the ideas.
4. For each barrier, discuss ways to overcome.
5. Commit to specific actions to overcome barriers if / when they arise.

Use the handout on the next page to track your group's ideas.

What Could Go Wrong?

Solution_____

What can we do to ensure we do not achieve the desired result?

1. _____

2. _____

3. _____

4. _____

5. _____

Ways to overcome barrier 1:

_____

Ways to overcome barrier 2:

_____

Ways to overcome barrier 3:

_____

Ways to overcome barrier 4:

_____

Ways to overcome barrier 5:

_____

About the Authors

Mary Scannell

A training consultant with 20 years of experience in developing, designing, and delivering training programs, Mary specializes in delivering high-value training that is cost effective and time efficient. She has worked with all levels of staff, from senior executives to entry-level employees. Known for her high-energy style, she attributes her ability to keep trainees engaged throughout the session to her use of the training activities found in this book.

Mary's expertise in games and group activities extends through the full gamut of the topic—from small classroom exercises to large-scale outdoor adventure events. She is an active member of her community, and for over a decade has worked with a local nonprofit to help Arizona youth become more connected to their schools, their homes, and their communities (educationalendeavors.com), through the use of experiential activities and ropes-course initiatives.

Mary is a member of the American Society for Training and Development. She received a B.S. from the W. P. Carey School of Business at Arizona State University.

Find out more about Mary Scannell at bizteamtools.com; or to contact Mary, call 602-663-7788 or email to mary@maryscannell.com.

Mike Mulvihill

Mike Mulvihill is the founder of PossibiliTEAMS, a team-building and training company offering fun and innovative team events to traditional corporate groups as well as virtual work teams around the globe. PossibiliTEAMS is the first company to offer a full lineup of team-building activities using virtual world technology. Mike has worked with teams throughout the United States, Europe, and Latin America, creating and facilitating team-building sessions for hundreds of organizations, ranging from Fortune 500 companies to small businesses, nonprofit groups, and government agencies.

Some of the clients Mike has worked with include Liberty Mutual Insurance, Pearson Digital Learning, Bank of America, McKinsey & Company, Charles Schwab, American Express, UPS, Motorola, Discover Financial Services, the Federal Highway Administration, and many more.

Mike is coauthor of *The Big Book of Virtual Team-Building Games* and is a member of the Society for Human Resource Management and the American Society for Training and Development. He received his bachelor's degree in organizational communication from Arizona State University.

Connect with Mike at PossibiliTEAMS at 888-225-3610, or by email at Mike@PossibiliTEAMS.com.